IN · A · VICTORIA
GARDEN

In · a · Victoria GARDEN

✦

Text and Photographs by

Lynne Milnes

ORCA BOOK PUBLISHERS

For Joe,
L. M.

Copyright © 1995 Lynne Milnes

Canadian Cataloguing in Publication Data
Milnes, Lynne, 1955–
In a Victoria garden

ISBN 1-55143-031-2
1. Gardens–British Columbia–Victoria.
2. Gardening–British Columbia–Victoria. I. Title.
SB466.C22V52 1995 635'.09711'28 C95–9102132

Publication assistance provided by The Canada Council.

Design by Christine Toller
All photographs by the author

Printed and bound in Hong Kong

Orca Book Publishers
PO Box 5626, Station B
Victoria, BC Canada
V8R 6S4

Orca Book Publishers
PO Box 468
Custer, WA USA
98240-0468

10 9 8 7 6 5 4 3 2 1

Table of Contents

The Gardens of

Author's Note

I began the cataloguing of Victoria's gardens five years ago, shortly after the birth of my daughter. Born three months too soon, Emma weighed in at a mere one-and-a-half pounds (760 grams to be exact). When she finally came home from the hospital three months later, full-time employment seemed out of the question, and yet I was faced with the hard reality of having to pay my share of the household expenses. I did not have a plan but I knew after spending three months in the hospital, and before that, three years in an office, that I wanted to be outside.

Along came a friend who offered to finance a fundraising calendar if I put it together. I was ecstatic and began my career as landscape photographer and garden snoop. The gardeners were gracious, hospitable and even offered to hold the baby so I could crawl around their gardens. While Emma slept I phoned potential retail outlets and researched printers, paper and format ideas.

Six months later, my friend left the city and I was left without any financing. But as time passed I built up a catalogue of Victoria gardens. My husband assured me that it was not only a good idea but a financially viable one. He encouraged my continuing research.

When spring arrived I had everything in place.

My husband financed the first printing and the *In A Victoria Garden* calendar was born. With Emma on my back I went out to sell.

The first year was a roaring success. Retailers were very supportive and Victoria tourists bought half the stock. The remaining calendars were sold to local Victorians for their friends and relatives back east and overseas and to the many locals who, like myself, dream about gardens year round.

Emma has just turned five and is ready to start kindergarten. The fourth calendar is out and I am in production on the next edition. This book became a natural extension of my chronicling of Victoria's gardens. As the gardeners passed on or moved I felt a growing urgency to catalogue their creative efforts. The interviews for *In A Victoria Garden* were given graciously over a period of a year. Some gardens required repeat visits in order to show seasonal and even annual variation or because I just didn't get it the first time.

I have one camera and one lens and do not own a tripod. Wind was and is a problem. I hope to continue to catalogue Victoria gardens every year. There are, I suspect, enough gardens and gardeners to last me a lifetime.

Lynne Milnes, February 1995

Introduction

Victoria, British Columbia, is a city of gardens situated on Vancouver Island at the extreme southwest coast of Canada. Blessed with a Mediterranean climate, a gardener in Victoria is able to enjoy cut flowers year round.

Retirees move to Victoria from all over Canada and the Pacific seaboard. They bring their wealth and leisure time which they devote to their homes and gardens. For the first time in their lives they begin to grow things. They specialize—alpines, roses, rhododendrons, native plants, dahlias, you name it, there is a society representing it, with hundreds of active members. They, in turn, bring busloads of visiting gardeners from all over the world to see and experience the ambience that is in a Victoria garden.

Every year millions of tourists visit the public gardens at Butchart, Beacon Hill Park and the Horticultural Centre of the Pacific. They ride in double-decker buses to peer at our beautiful city but are isolated from the people and private places that make this city so lovely.

Gardening is not just a "hobby" for Victorians but an intellectual pursuit which is studied, discussed, shared, and improved upon, year after year during a lifetime. It is an expression of creativity, an unheralded craft that is tapping the minds and imaginations of a growing number of people.

This book shows, with photographs and accompanying text, years of dedication from a select group of Victorians who have a passion for gardening.

The Garden of Pierre Archambault and Brent Webber

I first met Brent Webber over the phone. I was trying to identify an old rose that had been planted in the 1920s. I went to several local rosarians and we pored over books without success. Then I phoned Brent. He asked me several questions: "Are the leaves a dark green or light? Are they pointed or serrated? When was it planted? Is the bud a pink apricot blushing out to a pale golden colour?" Within a few minutes Brent had determined that the name of the rose was 'Paul Lédé.'

What I didn't know then was that Brent had become blind. He died four months later, but his

*R*ose-covered gateways connect this garden to the neighbours' where plants are shared back and forth, including the scented yellow climbing rose 'Goldfinch' and the pink R. 'Fragrant Pillar.' Chinese pots of succulents complete the scene.

gardening legacy lives on. His partner, Pierre Archambault, maintains their beautifully restored Victorian house and garden. Pierre remembers Brent as the plant designer.

"He knew his plant material," recalls Pierre. "He read every book on gardening that he could get from cover to cover, absorbing everything. While I was more hesitant about colour selections, Brent knew right away which colours worked. He designed the original colour scheme of mauve, yellow, and pink."

Pierre, with his charming French accent, chuckles, "Brent had an eye."

When Pierre Archambault came to Victoria from Montreal in 1975, he thought he would stay for the summer. But like many easterners he was captivated by the beauty of the city and the Mediterranean climate. Reluctant at first to sell his business in Montreal, he found a job in Victoria within a day and that was it.

In 1978 Pierre and Brent bought their present house and began the task of creating a garden. It wasn't easy. The ground was wet and mossy; drainage was poor. As a result, Brent and Pierre dug up the soil and brought in topsoil. They kept the old fruit trees but every year their perennial beds got bigger and bigger and slowly the grass was replaced by slate paving and brick. Because they had so much new topsoil they made raised vegetable beds. Pierre still remembers plant colour and texture even when planting vegetables. His raised beds are designed each year with different colours of lettuce and herbs. Rows of artichokes, kohlrabi, leeks, and broad beans are arranged artistically with an eye for colour and height. He grows many varieties of vegetables from Territorial Seeds Ltd., which would not be able to grow in his native Montreal. Keeping to his European heritage he also grows French bush beans, tomatoes, and peas.

"I keep adding more flowers every year. Last year I had huge clumps of Sweet William and gladiolas among the garlic and onions. It looked wonderful," he states.

Pierre and Brent always shared their plants with their neighbour, Shirley Beach. If Shirley found a rose in a ditch, she would take two cuttings—one for her own garden and one for Pierre

*M*ost gardeners stay away from the colour orange in the garden, but not Brent and Pierre. They accent an orange-tipped Euphorbia with bronze fennel, yellow allium, a rusty-tinged ornamental grass and an ivory-coloured azalea.

and Brent's. It worked both ways and soon the two gardens were joined by a path and rose-covered gateway.

"It made our exchanges easier," smiles Pierre. "Shirley gave us the yellow Goldfinch climbing rose by the gate and the pink fragrant pillar came from a cutting which we gave to her." They both share the pale pink aromatic old rose, 'Cécile Brunner.'

Pierre and Brent used climbers as fences until neighbours and friends helped them build a fence. Then they grew a succession of roses intertwined with clematis such as *C. texensis*, a late-flowering deep red variety with tulip-like flowers. Pierre has an exceptional collection of succulents which he acquired over time by trading with friends and interested members of the Victoria Horticultural Society's Hardy Plant Group. Pierre has been a member of this serious gardening collective since he came to the city. He uses his greenhouse to overwinter bromeliads and the tender succulents that need protection from frost. But even in winter this garden has something to offer.

I asked Pierre the story of his unusual statuary, which is outside all year. His Chinese lion came from a shop in Victoria's Chinatown. The shop owner didn't want to sell it but Pierre persisted and now, in the late spring, it sits in oriental splendour among pale pink peonies, purple flag iris, and cerulean blue tradescantia. It is a focal point for this planting, creating a sense of intimacy. The cement lion with raised paw is surrounded by the lush green foliage of the peony, while surrounding roses and clematis continue to flower after the peony has finished.

Another exceptional planting features a lady-with-mirror statue. It came from his friend Rosemary Wells, an antiquarian who brought it carefully on her lap from England. When she sold her house and moved into an apartment, she gave Pierre the statue as long as she could have "visiting rights." The statue sits amid a backdrop of orange-tipped euphorbias and feathery bronze fennel. Orange is often a difficult colour to incorporate in a garden but Brent designed this planting to complement the orange colour rather than fight it. Yellow iris, golden-flowered onions, ivory-coloured azalea and even a rust-tinged ornamental grass all work together to complete the picture.

The last time I chatted with Pierre we were in his kitchen, recently painted a bright yellow as a backdrop for his collection of French blue and white china. It was like the Impressionist painter Monet's kitchen and I felt transported to another place and time. Who should come over at that moment but Rosemary Wells, to "visit" her statue and have a walk with Pierre through his charming garden.

Postscript: Pierre died in August, 1994, and his house and garden have been sold.

*P*ierre Archambault's Chinese lion is surrounded by pale pink peonies, blue tradescantia, clematis 'Ville de Lyon' and, in the foreground, bearded iris.

The Garden of Les and Shirley Beach

*O*ver one hundred scented roses climb on homemade rustic arbours. Romantic statuary such as this "Romeo and Juliet" figure give the garden its intimate ambience.

You can smell the garden of Les and Shirley Beach before you see it. Waves of perfume from the more than one hundred old roses mingle in the air from the sidewalk. Upon entering the garden you see the pale pink Bourbon rose 'Kathleen Harrop' draped over the verandah.

To your right is an arbour of the highly scented climbing rose 'Alchymist' intertwined with the vine *Jasmine beesianum*; the hybrid musk rose 'Pax' grows beside a charming statue of lovers. On your left is a curved bench from which to view the carefully restored heritage house and

Shirley Beach's favourite rose, the deep red-purple gallica Rosa 'Charles de Mills' has a musky scent.

the creative tangle that surrounds it.

"This was an empty lot," said Les, pointing to the twenty-five-foot strip that is now the main focus of the garden. "When we came here in 1973 from Rossland, B.C., this was a mess of broken glass, wire, and rubble. The house was covered with asbestos shingles but we knew there was a gem underneath." Les and Shirley spent the first few years on their Hallmark Society award-winning restoration of the turn-of-the-century house. In 1976 they raised the house four feet to put in a basement and found it supported on brick pillars. The bricks became the beginning of brick paths for the newly acquired narrow lot next door.

At this time Shirley wrote to Sunningdale in Surrey, England, for an order of fifty old roses that she had read about in C. L. Lucas Philips' book, *Roses for the Small Garden*. This began a passion which has made the Beaches' garden famous throughout Canada. It was featured on the cover of Nicole Eaton's *In a Canadian Garden*, included in Marjorie Harris' *The Canadian Gardener* and in Rodale's *Illustrated Encyclopedia of Perennials*, not to mention numerous magazine articles.

"We've never had a plan," said Shirley, "but we have made definite 'rooms' separated by Les' rustic arbours and narrow grass paths." Where once a driveway existed, the Beaches have planted a thyme carpet with hardy geraniums and self-seeded campanula. The David Austen rose 'Constance Spry' arches gracefully over the carpet with the pale yellow, sweet-smelling rambling rose 'Goldfinch' grown from a cutting which she shared with her neighbour and gardening enthusiast, Pierre Archambault. Both gardens are now joined by a common rose arbour and their gardens are an annual feature on the Victoria Horticultural Society and the Hardy Plant Group tours.

Shirley is also a member of an old-rose group. "We're a funny bunch," she laughed. "None of us drive, we all love cats, and we aren't afraid to let plants self-seed so that we can share seedlings." They also share cuttings, mail orders, successes, and failures. "David Austen roses have never done well in my garden but maybe it is because of the wind hitting the house. Pierre's garden, behind us, is much warmer. You must constantly be aware of your own garden's limits."

Beyond the thyme carpet is a large urn edged with santolina, spilling over the brick paving. From here you can enter a succession of "rooms" featuring lovely bronze miniatures raised on pedestals and surrounded by an interesting mixture of angelica, lavender, astrantia, white borage, hardy geraniums, and boxwood. The Beaches use small trees such as yews, cedars, monkey puzzle, and standardized flowering quince for vertical interest. The rest of the garden is a profusion of colour.

"We tend to shy away from oranges," said Shirley. "With roses, the softer pinks and pale yellows are more prevalent, although my favourite is the deep red-purple gallica, 'Charles de Mills,' with a musky scent." For Les it is 'Mme Hardy,' a white Damask rose with vigorous growth. "It doesn't bloom all that well," he explained, "but I like its foliage."

The Beaches do not spray their roses, choosing instead to grow varieties that are disease resistant. "Often the foliage looks terrible while the roses are blooming, particularly 'May Gold' and 'Leverkusen.'" The Beaches cut the roses back hard after they flower and again in the fall. They water with soaker hoses regularly and only use an overhead sprinkler if it is particularly dry. Mulching is done with compost and an annual feed of cow or horse manure. They have many birds that eat the caterpillars and aphids but snails are a problem. Snails like to climb and raccoons like the snails, which makes a mess of the arbours. "But," said Shirley, "this year we had a nest of robins in the *Clematis armandii* by the front door and four young were raised successfully without interference by cats or raccoons."

Butterflies are also seen in the garden. The afternoon I visited, a yellow and black swallowtail darted about a perennial border of white peony ('Flava Maxima'), yellow Jerusalem sage, bearded iris, sweet rocket, lavatera, *Geranium phaeum*, and self-seeded hollyhocks beside the primrose-scented evergreen rose 'Adélaide d'Orléans.' Against the fence is a quaint two-seater arbour with *Akebia quinata*, obtained as a cutting from gardener Doris

A quiet corner in the garden of Les and Shirley Beach with a line from Gertrude Stein on the watering can.

Page. Its deep maroon flowers hang down over the vine-covered benches. Nearby, *Clematis viticella purpurea plena elegans* blooms with huge lavender-coloured flowers. Along the back verandah is the fruity-smelling mock orange 'Belle Etoille' and roses gallica 'Great Maiden's Blush' and rambler 'Dr. W. van Fleet.'

In the back corner is a sitting bench with a thyme carpet, and self-seeded pink columbine 'Nora Barlow' between a box hedge. Behind it the vigorous apple-scented rose 'Albertine' climbs along the fence next to the deep pink 'Zépherine Drouhin' and 'Blairii No. 2.' An abutilon was in bloom on the side garden beside the rambler 'Ayrshire Splendens,' which smelled of myrrh. Under a pergola of laburnum is the unusual *Kalacanthus floridus*, whose scent resembles fermenting apple cider, a yeasty alcoholic aroma.

Feeling very heady and overwhelmed by the sensual experience of Les and Shirley Beach's garden, I left by the front entrance covered in the cream-coloured, silky-scented rose 'Gloire de Dijon.' Even after I closed the gate, the scent lingered.

The Garden of Annabeth and David Black

*D*avid and Annabeth Black are committed to maintaining the mature canopy of their waterfront estate, "Riffington." Under a Japanese maple a carpet of native lilies, Erythronium oreganum *greets the spring.*

Annabeth Black is very serious about conserving the heritage value of "Riffington," the waterfront mansion that she and her family moved to in 1986. "With a property this size, our big worry is how to maintain a beautiful canopy."

Riffington was designed by Vancouver archi- tect Philip Julien, and built in 1913 for Andrew Wright, one of the early developers of the Up- lands, Victoria's most prestigious residential area. Wright was an owner of the Lansdowne Floral Company and he had a keen interest in landscape design. It is thought that the original landscape ar-

*A*gainst the granite walls of the estate, an espaliered flowering quince, Chaenomeles x superba, *blooms in early spring.*

chitect for the estate was Olmstead and Sons because of the curved driveway and laurel hedges, their trademark, but there are no written records to verify this. From 1928 to 1942 the house, boasting eight fireplaces, was used as a United States consulate with such illustrious guests as the Duke of Kent and Princess Margaret. The gardens are equally impressive with enormous native Douglas fir trees and two heritage horticultural features, a century-old blue Lebanon cedar and a weeping sequoia.

"We have tree work done every other year," Annabeth explained, "but I still worry about the future of these enormous firs." The trees were topped in the 1970s, which may shorten their lifespan as the prevailing winds are fierce. "Last year we lost a huge oak and cypress tree due to wind. We brought in a small mill and used the planks to repair a foot bridge. The *Arbutus unedo* was killed to the ground twice but I'm still hoping it will come back again."

On a tour through the garden Annabeth pointed out some of the changes to the landscaping over the last eight years. "Coming from the interior I wasn't sure at first about the growing conditions. For the first year I concentrated on maintaining what we had." With four children at home, and a busy social calendar, Annabeth was also left with three-and-a-half acres of beachfront property, most of which is under cultivation. The garden had been beautifully maintained by full-time gardener, John Ritz. "For the first year the new gardener and I didn't make many changes. We just tried to learn as much as we could about the garden and its plants.

"Over time, David has added sprinkler systems to the large beds. Come and look," said Annabeth, pointing to a group of rhododendrons in bud for the first time in the shady north side facing Beach Drive. "I planted three fragrant *Rhododendron* 'Loderi' along with the three yews and one hundred heathers. The garden is so large that it is important to plant in large drifts. I am slowly learning how to do this," admitted Annabeth. Trained as a master gardener at the Van Dusen Gardens in Vancouver, Annabeth sits on the board of the municipal Parks and Recreation

Commission. She also writes a weekly gardening column for her husband's Island News Group, a local paper. "I am always learning," she said.

Walking along the circular drive, Annabeth pointed out the perennials that have been added. "I have transplanted hellebore seedlings throughout the garden and they seem to be doing very well. At first I planted large rhododendrons to fill in gaps but now I am using more and more native material such as kinnickinnick, *Arctostaphylos uva-ursi*, and evergreen huckleberries (*Vaccinium ovatum*)." Native plants are more tolerant of the extreme winds and offer more than just spring interest. "I try whenever I can to save native seeds and scatter them. It seems to be working. There are more chocolate lilies [*Fritillaria lanceolata*] and fawn lilies [*Erythronium oregonum*]. The native bleeding heart, *Dicentra formosa*, is a bit of a pest but there are a few places where I let it take over. However, the introduced trailing blackberry and English ivy are very invasive and are discouraged."

By the Japanese pond, Annabeth pointed out where she has added more azaleas to complete the existing planting of Japanese maples, Chinese wisteria, and irises. Down the stone steps to the waterfront perennial borders, Annabeth is less than satisfied. "Every year I add more bulbs, but in the summer the beds are thick with daylilies and self-seeded foxgloves. I need to do more work here. We took out the carpet annual beds on the water side. We thought the magnificent sea view and mountains were enough. Under the shore pines I've planted sweet woodruff which does well, but I still need more of a wind break right on the water's edge. We've tried Mugo pines without success. I'm thinking of the native ocean spray, *Holodiscus discolor*."

Walking from the sea under the great Garry oaks towards the house, Annabeth pointed out where she has cut back the shrubs that hid the house. "I'm also trying to get rid of the tea roses. I don't like to spray and they seem to need constant attention. Over time I would prefer more shrub roses."

Annabeth showed me her seedlings and cuttings in the original greenhouse. "I usually heel

In the cutting garden the Black children erected a scarecrow to fend off marauding crows from the family strawberry patch. Against the wall is the climber Rosa 'Sovereign.'

new plants in the cutting garden because it is more sheltered before moving them to the outer perennial borders. I love the vegetable garden. It has been worked for almost a century. We grow strawberries, raspberries, lettuce, corn, potatoes and, of course, tomatoes in the greenhouse. I found the roots of a very old yellow concorde grape with the root outside the greenhouse and then added a red 'Flame' with the root inside. Both vines pro-duce well and the grapes are delicious."

Annabeth and David Black do worry about the future of their Riffington garden, but they are committed to planting trees. "I want to leave a leg-acy of native trees," explained Annabeth, showing her seedlings of arbutus, Douglas fir, Garry oak and shore pine. "As the mature trees die we have a responsibility to leave something in their place."

The Garden of Lord and Lady Chatfield

L ord and Lady Chatfield created this world-class garden in four years with the help of landscape consultant Cyril Hume. The red 'American Pillar' rose blooms on the trellis while the soft yellow mounds of lady's-mantle edge the perennial border. It includes hardy geraniums, golden yarrow, early white chrysanthemum, campanula and a deep-blue Anchusa*.*

The best part of living on the West Coast," said Elizabeth Chatfield between sips of her India tea, "is the smell of wet earth every month of the year. In eastern Canada you would be lucky to be able to work in the soil for six months, but here, there are flowers through-out the year." We looked out the window to the flower-studded spring garden beyond.

Down a country lane, one block from the ocean and the blustery winds of the Strait of Juan de Fuca, is the "restful" garden of Lord and Lady Chatfield. Visitors describe it as restful because it

Beside the exposed bedrock Lady Chatfield designed a grey garden. Surrounding the sundial are woolly thyme, lamb's ears, sage, lavendar and ornamental grasses.

looks as though it has always been there, although the Chatfields only started clearing the site four years ago.

"We cleared the garden for three months," explained Ernle Chatfield as he sipped his China tea. "The English ivy which had grown up forty feet in all the Garry oaks had to be removed or the trees would die; however, the mature rhododendrons, the pond and the seven standpipes for watering all attest to the fact that there was once a beautiful garden." But it had become so wild the Chatfields employed a surveyor to find the lot lines—not even the neighbours were sure of their location. They then built a chain link fence for Vennie, their rambunctious almost-German shepherd dog. "We had to fence, of course," explained Lord Chatfield, "but the clematises have done splendidly and they've almost covered it." Clematis 'Nelly Moser,' C. tangutica, C. 'Margaret Hunt', C. 'Vyvyan Pennell,' C. 'Etoile Violette', C. macropetala, and C. montana climb along the fence while C. 'Ville de Lyon' climbs through the roses on the arbour.

The Chatfields brought in many yards of manure, soil, and gravel to build their garden and the growth has been tremendous. A rose, accidentally broken during the Conservatory of Music fundraising garden tour, recovered admirably, growing thirty more feet up a tree that season. On the advice of landscape consultant Cyril Hume, they extended their rose pergola from the front of the garden to the back garden gate. Rosa splendens grows along the fence and pergola with R. 'Viking Queen.' Halfway along, under the dramatic red R. 'American Pillar' is a wooden bench that overlooks the perennial borders carefully planted between two outcrops of exposed bedrock. Cyril used fine gravel for the wide paths but softened the edges with billowy blooms of lady's-mantle and perennial geraniums. On the rocks, gentians, succulents, and other alpines are carefully placed in rock crevices. Invasive ground cover such as lily-of-the-valley, polygonum, and houttuynia grow between the rocks to keep them confined. These "rivers" of green work beautifully against the rough texture of the exposed granite.

Lady Chatfield planned a silver-grey garden

near the beginning of the pergola. Around a sundial on the flat, sun-baked rock is a silver leaf pear and plantings of lavender, sage and lamb's ears. Across the lawn and under the oaks is the shady woodland garden with rhododendrons, azaleas, masses of bulbs and shade-tolerant perennials such as Himalayan poppies and epimedium. The Chatfields are careful not to use glaring colours which might foreshorten the view of the garden from the house. What you see is the spectacular perennial border and pergola on one side and the rolling woodland garden on the other, leading to a rocky mount. At its base is a little pond built by the original owners. The Chatfields added a waterfall over the rocks, which improves aeration for the goldfish. "Wild ducks visit the pond," exclaimed Lord Chatfield with obvious delight.

After tea, we wandered through the garden, past the pond and up the rocky bluff or "Vennie's Mount," so named for the ever-zealous dog bouncing from one person to another. The Chatfields were relaxed as he bounded through and on the knot garden. They admitted that Vennie was hard on the garden but they explained that as a member of the family he was entitled to share it. Cyril Hume looks after most of the maintenance, one day a week; the Chatfields thus have time for other activities, including the Victoria Horticultural Society, in which they are both active members.

Climbing up the stone steps built into the rocks, we passed new plantings of Romneya coulteri, the California tree poppy, and Limnanthes seeding itself among the different species of broom. Lord and Lady Chatfield pointed out their future projects. Cyril plans to make a woodland walk through the rhododendrons and he is always looking in nurseries for items on the Chatfields' wish list. "They are special people," he said, obviously enjoying the creative collaboration as much as they do.

We paused at the front gate, near to the kitchen and cutting garden. "The vegetable plot used to be in the centre of the lawn but we filled that in. I missed fresh vegetables, so Cyril suggested a small ornamental plot here," explained Lady Chatfield. The use of ornamental arches for training runner

The Chatfields uncovered a pond in a heap of brambles to which they added a waterfall, irises and water lilies.

beans adds vertical interest. "It is small but we manage to fit in rhubarb, strawberries, currants, espalier apples 'Liberty' and 'Jonafree,' asparagus, beans, and a few tomatoes. Of course," said Lady Chatfield, "unlike Ontario, you cannot get a decent tasting tomato to grow here. The nights are too cold." But she and Lord Chatfield do not appear to mind.

The Garden of Bob Clarke

A Buddha ponders the changing seasons in Bob Clarke's Japanese-style garden.

When Bob Clarke's son got married he told his father he wanted to have the wedding ceremony in his father's Japanese garden "...so you had better get busy and build it." Bob said he had dreamed about it for years. "It was a bit makeshift at first," he admitted, "but it was the beginning of this garden."

Twenty years later the garden is still being refined with new rock paths, crushed gravel "seas," and "island" beds of interesting plants. It was designed around viewing platforms: from the swimming pool attached to the deck, from the

Wood, stone and foliage are essential elements in this garden. Bob first carved the rain catcher at the edge of his teahouse in wood. Later, he had it cast in concrete.

waiting bench looking back towards the house, and from the Japanese-style teahouse at the bottom of the garden.

When Bob's children were young, the yard was mostly lawn with exposed rock outcroppings. It was Bob's fascination with the natural rock that gave him the idea for the Japanese-style ponds and stream. He built the teahouse for the kids to play in and have sleep-outs in. Now Bob's grandchildren play in the garden and swim in the covered pool.

For privacy, he has built shingle-capped fences with "privacy panels" depicting Japanese scenes. Lighting is as important in this garden as plants, and Bob admitted he takes as much pleasure in the garden at night as he does during the day. "At least at night you don't see the weeds," he laughed. Statuary is also very important and Bob has a strategically placed Buddha and his own hand-made thirteen-storey tower. He also carved a rain catcher out of wood to catch the run-off from the teahouse roof. He has since had it cast in concrete but it still retains the hand-made look. "I like unique items in the garden," he said.

The front of the Clarke residence is mostly fragrant roses, annuals, and a beautiful sculptural mound of *Cotoneaster prostratus* 'Dammeri' with its evergreen foliage, white spring flowers, and red berries in the fall. From the driveway you enter the Japanese-style garden through a covered gate with a lovely hummingbird motif carved in it. Down the narrow hand-picked pebble path to the back garden your eye is always drawn to the next vista.

A wooden bridge takes you to an island planting of Scotch moss, *Euonymus japonicus*, *Hakonechloa macra* 'Aureola,' a horizontal yew (*Juniperus horizontalis*), *Potentilla* x *tonguei*, and Japanese umbrella pine (*Sciadopitys verticillata*). Within the adjacent island is Japanese bloodgrass (*Imperata cylindrica*) and several varieties of Japanese maples with intricately cut leaves. A flowering *Prunus serrulata* 'Kwanson' will eventually shade this area of the garden.

Looking towards the teahouse you can see flowering azaleas and *Robinia pseudoacacia* under a canopy of a magnificent Atlas cedar tree, *Cedrus atlantica*. Bob uses sempervivums among the rocks and gravel for textural accent, and bamboo around the perimeter where privacy is required. He is just starting to add various species of clematis on the border fencing of the garden.

Behind the azaleas the garden slopes down towards the teahouse where dwarf Japanese maples spill over the rocks in a foliage "waterfall." There is red-leafed *Acer palmatum* 'Dissectum Atropurpureum' and green-leafed *A.p.* 'Corallinum,' both of which turn brilliant red and orange in the fall. In the shade, native sword ferns and ostrich ferns thrive. Because of his hilltop location, wind is a problem—especially when trying to establish tender new plants, such as the choice paperbark maple, *Acer griseum*. However, Bob is not discouraged. Like any dedicated gardener, he hopes for success next year.

Bob admitted he is not a garden expert. He worked for thirty-five years at B.C. Forests Products as a sawyer and retired seven years ago. Since then he has designed and built ten other Japanese-style gardens and currently maintains eight gardens besides his own. A devoted father and grandfather, Bob has put together books of quotations for each of his grandchildren using his own calligraphy. A poet in his free time, Bob has a binder full of his musings that he often shares with members of the Victoria Horticultural Society of which he is an active member, having been head of the Garden Visit Program and the Camera Club for two years.

This summer, Bob is building two Japanese viewing gardens for major public garden shows. He and his wife visited Japan for three weeks in 1977 and since then have hosted forty-five Japanese students. He is the president of the Takata Japanese Garden Society, a group that is dedicated to restoring the Japanese gardens along the Gorge waterway. "I've always had a fascination with things Japanese," admitted Bob.

In addition to all of these community involvements, Bob is also writing a book. "I'm in an enviable position," he said. "I can do things on my own time in my own way." Right now he is busy making changes to his teahouse in time for his youngest son's wedding ceremony, to be held in the garden.

The contrasting foliage of bamboo, Japanese maples, cotoneaster and ferns is the focus of this rockery.

The Garden of Anne and Derek Cooper

*D*rs. Anne and Derek Cooper have turned a garden shed into an attractive feature with the deep yellow flowers of climbing Fremontia californica *and the aromatic apricot-coloured rose* 'Paul Lédé' *beside Deutzia, bleeding hearts, and hellebores.*

When Anne Cooper first saw the view from her Deep Cove property she knew right away. "This is it!" she exclaimed. Eight years later she and her husband, Derek, have completely renovated the old beach house and created a charming English cottage garden.

They began by ripping up everything. Heavy machinery was needed for the construction work. By the time they finished, the front yard was a flat sea of mud. They kept an old ornamental plum tree and a few plants but removed the diseased fruit trees. A plain cedar fence was built

In one corner of the front gate, Anne has planted a beautiful combination of white Campanula pakesimana, *pink* Dianthus 'Doris', *frothy white* Omphalodes linifolia *and the tiny pink* Diascia vigilis.

for privacy, and architect Pamela Charlesworth designed a wide brick curved path. "I wanted a straight path," remembered Anne. "But Pamela insisted, and of course she was absolutely right." The path meanders from the front gate to the back deck, surrounded by perennial borders, potted plants, and climbing roses.

On the seaside deck, roses 'Felicite et Perpétue' and 'Golden Showers' climbs against the trellis beside alpine trough gardens with miniature pines, androsace, anemones, and sempervivums. Trailing down the steep bank to the sea are St-John's-wort, thimbleberries, honeysuckle, lemon balm with golden hops climbing over a seaside gazebo and sea buckthorn with blue-green leaves. A beautiful pale blue Ceanothus 'Gloire de Versailles' frames part of the deck with a pink form on the path side, next to a hot pink Damask rose 'Jenny Duval' that fades to pale mauve as it ages. A spectacular red rose 'Europeana' climbs the woodshed leading to the front slate patio past Anne's potting shed.

Anne is an active propagator and grows seeds collected from the Victoria Horticultural Society, the Vancouver Island Rock and Alpine Growers Society, the British Hardy Plant Group and the American Alpine Society. This year she grew 150 different varieties of plants from seed with an eighty percent success rate. The evidence of her work was everywhere. Little pots of seedlings covered her potting area, patio, paths, and greenhouse. She has even commandeered her husband's vegetable patch for fledgling plants and trial specimens.

"When we started this garden, my husband and I were both working as doctors. I would go to nurseries or garden clubs, buy plants, and race home after work and shove them in. Of course I tried to keep the tall plants at the back and shorter material at the front but...," Anne laughed. "You can see that sometimes I failed completely. I am fond of green flowering plants or white and creamy flowers but it can look too wishy-washy. I counteract this with scarlet such as Geum 'Mrs. Bradshaw' and Crocosmia 'Lucifer.' Now that I am retired from medicine I have more time to consider a plant's needs." Anne is constantly adding,

moving, and rearranging the plants in the garden.

She has built a new rose arbour from her patio with scented climbers 'Tiffany' and 'Alchymist' amid Akebia quinata and Clematis alpina 'Helsingborg.' Hybrid musk roses such as pale pink 'Sally Homes' and a white 'Mediland' flank the rockery, along with hardy geraniums, yellow Lavandula viridis, yellow-leafed caryopteris, santolina, blue campanula, and the very unusual blue-tinged Cerinthe major. Against the fence the Damask moss rose 'Fantin-Latour' climbs with purple Clematis jackmanii behind a border of sedges, yellow-leafed aquilegia 'Roman Bronze,' and a selection of euphorbias: E. amygdaloides subsp. robbiae, E. palustris, E. rigida, and E. mollis 'Chameleon.'

The colours along the border change from yellow to orange with Potentilla fruticosa 'Red ace,' Hemerocallis fulva 'Kwanso Flore Plena,' and red Crocosmia 'Lucifer' against a background of thalictrums, Physostegia virginiana, Astrantia maxima, and Astrantia major which Anne lets seed. She is not afraid to use vibrant colours and one planter of brilliant orange-pink schizanthus with bronze and orange salpiglossis caught my eye.

Across the path against the garage is the salmon-pink scented rose 'Just Joey' with yellow Clematis tangutica and orange kniphofia. In the foreground, Lysimachia ephemerum, hybrid musk rose 'Ballerina,' and Geranium versicolour vie for space. Anne uses clematis throughout the garden. Clematis texensis 'Pagoda' grows on and through the box hedge, while Clematis texensis 'Duchess of Albany' grows in the small bridal wreath tree, Sturay japonica. The double-purple Clematis viticella purpurea plena elegans grows in a vibernum opposite a deep pink Clematis viticella 'Abundance' entwined in a dwarf cherry. The garden is layered with plants for colour and foliage interest throughout the year.

Beside the garage, architect Pamela Charlesworth built an arbour (now covered in honeysuckle) with a wooden bench to separate the perennial borders. The Coopers use this spot for potted impatiens beside a pale pink fuschia. By the front gate is the wintersweet shrub, Anne's favourite, with a border of sedums, pussy-toes, dianthus, heuchera, and the

Beside the ocean-front gate Ceanothus *'Gloire de Versailles,' both blue and pink forms, grows next to hot pink Damask rose 'Jenny Duval.'*

splendid red-flowered *Zauschneria californica* 'Glasnevin' on one side; the semi-evergreen shrub *Zenobia pulverulenta*, *Dicentra* 'Stuart Boothman,' purple sedum, variegated yellow columbine, and the delicate white annual *Omphalodes linifolia* make a fine display on the other.

The Coopers have to garden on clay soil. They brought in yards and yards of topsoil to make the garden, and add annual feedings of cow manure or mushroom manure topped up with generous layers of leaf mulch from Beacon Hill Park. They share a fence and climbing plants with a neighbour who also loves to garden, and if their water runs out the neighbour has a well they can draw from for their hoses. Derek wanted a lawn and he does not mind tending it under the old ornamental plum. It is a perfect spot for snoozing in the shade.

Before I left, I returned to the deck and watched a heron fishing off the point as a sailboat passed. In the breeze, I smelled the sea and sweet scent of roses just as the first drops of rain began to fall.

The Garden of Beryl and Dick Edgell

*M*rs. Owen-Flood inherited this garden which was once part of the Edgell estate. True to the original planting, she has maintained these gorgeous candelabra primulas as foreground to flowering azaleas and a double-flowering, deep-purple French lilac.

The Uplands garden of Dick and Beryl Edgell was famous in its day. Featured in a 1948 issue of *House and Garden* magazine and a 1949 issue of *Canadian Homes and Gardens*, the garden personified the Edgells' commitment to their home and family.

The house was built in 1936 by Mr. Lancelot McCulloch, brother of Mrs. Edgell, and husband of the late Sybil McCulloch, an important figure in the Victoria gardening community. Old photographs of the area show it as flat pasture land without the large native Garry oaks and ornamen-

Underneath the magnificent rhododendrons is an understory of naturalized anemones (both single, double, pink and white), native easter lilies and even a white form of chocolate lily.

tal trees that we see today.

Gillian Stewart, the Edgells' younger daughter, remembers growing up in a household whose yard was unfenced and where cows wandered freely. "I remember being terrified that I would meet a wild cow as I walked home from the streetcar roundabout." The Edgells bought and ploughed the lot behind their house, which included a high rock outcrop and two natural pools. They built another Japanese-style pool in the front garden surrounded by Japanese maples and a juniper trimmed in Japanese "cloud" forms.

"My mother loved foliage colour in trees. She planted willows next to copper beech, pin oaks [*Quercus palustris*] and many different species of maples," said Gillian. "We went on plant collecting expeditions to Cowichan to bring back native ferns and pink lilies [*Erythronium revolutum*] which have since crossed with the white lilies [*E. oregonum*] to produce a pale pink form. My parents were avid members of the Rock and Alpine Society and the Rhododendron Society. Rhododendrons were the big draw to gardens in the '40s and '50s. My parents bought plants from Allan Goddard, Mary Grieg, Ed Lohbrunner, and Layritz Nursery. They traded plants with rhododendron propagators Stuart Holland and Albert de Mezey, who actually named one of his new hybrids 'Beryl Edgell.'"

Beryl had a superb eye for detail and it was she who designed the perimeter plantings of large flowering shrubs (*Hydrangea aspera* subsp. *aspera*, *Syringa* 'Charles Joly,' and azaleas) with underplantings of native fawn lilies, chocolate lilies, anemones, trilliums, and cultivated candelabra primulas. She liked paths to curve and surprise the viewer and her plantings were designed so they could be viewed from many angles.

In the style of the day, it was very much a spring garden. Once the rhododendrons and azaleas had finished, there were formal summer plantings of Regal lilies and hybrid tea roses with annuals planted in large urns on the Virginia blue slate terrace. The vegetable garden produced food for the family all year and they supplied lily-of-the-valley to florists in California for shipment to France for the Muguet des bois celebration on the first of May. This tradition continues to this day but the plants are now shipped to Montreal.

"My parents loved to share the garden. There were always people coming over and trading plants. That is how they learned—from each other. In the '50s they entertained and I remember my dad saying he didn't mind the girdled ladies in their front shirt-waist dresses and spiked high heels because they aerated the lawn. My father was the alpine grower. He had a scree garden at the top of the rocks with tiny alpines he traded and collected. By the time he died, the surrounding trees had grown up and shaded the once-sunny rockery and it was too hard to maintain. It is now a bed of candelabra primulas."

Mr. and Mrs. Stewart moved back to the family home in 1968 after the death of Mr. Edgell. They built a house on top of the rocks in the back lot for Mrs. Edgell where she lived until 1988. "We maintained the garden the way it was until mom died. I was raising my own children and I never felt like it was really my own garden until then," said Gillian. When Mrs. Edgell's house was sold to Mrs. Owen-Flood, the garden was divided and a low fence with a wrought iron gate was built between the two gardens, which changed the focus and sense of space of the original garden.

Since then, Gillian has removed the hybrid tea roses that required spraying and added perennials. She has made her own white garden under the shade of a copper beech with white forms of meadowsweet (*Filipendula ulmaria* 'Aurea'), primula (*Primula japonica* 'Postford White'), gillenia, tradescantia, gentian, acanthus, maidenhair fern, bleeding heart, crambe, heuchera, hostas (*Hosta sieboldii, H. fortunei, H. hypoleuca*), hydrangea (*Hydrangea gigantica*), Casablanca lilies, and clematis ('Mme le Coultre') growing up through an old fragrant azalea. Gillian has incorporated statuary and ferns from her late aunt Sybil's garden. "Sybil's *Cardiocrinum giganteum* is in the white garden and I have her cement Japanese temple surrounded by her fern collection in a shady spot."

Gillian has divided her perennial colours further with a blue and yellow border of *Euphorbia*

*G*illian Stewart has added a colourful assortment of perennials to what was once, in her parents' day, a formal rose garden.

seguieriana, coreopsis, thalictrums, eringiums, gillenia, and tradescantia, while the more romantic pinks of peonies and astrantias are combined with old roses below the rose arbour.

Plans are underway for more changes in the garden but Gillian is always sensitive to the original design of her parents. Her sister, Susan Ryley, is also a serious gardener, and Gillian's own daughter, Susan, is just starting her first garden. Gillian was thrilled to help her daughter and pass on the family gardening tradition to the next generation.

The Garden of Elizabeth England

*E*lizabeth England is a true colourist. She paints pictures with flowers. Shown here, grey lamb's ears, Lychnis, *feverfew,* Allium christophii, *a blue bearded iris,* Filipendula camtschatica *in front of the pink Bourbon rose 'Zéphirine Drouhin.'*

*I*magine a woman with an extensive collection of WHO memorabilia mounted on her dining room wall, next to a portrait of Queen Victoria and a bookcase full of gardening books. Elizabeth England, librarian and collector, knows what she likes, from rock music to plant foliage, and she displays it decoratively and artistically with an individualistic sense of style.

"I know I am opinionated," she laughed. "I love what I love and I hate what I hate. But how can you develop your own sense of style unless you have strong opinions?" Her garden does not appeal to

*M*artagon lilies and yellow dwarf bamboo do well in the shade in Elizabeth's backyard "island" beds.

everyone. "Men do not seem to see what I am doing, but women more often understand that I have built it, bit by bit," said Elizabeth, poring over her enormous scrapbook of plant labels and seed packets.

Elizabeth moved to her Oak Bay house in 1969 with her professor husband and her two children in diapers. She did what she could to clear the long-abandoned garden and started reading. When her children were school age she worked part-time as a gardener for an American woman in the Uplands. The woman wanted colour throughout the garden in all seasons. The more colour she added to the Uplands garden, the more Elizabeth turned away from colour in her own garden. She focused on foliage and read books by Beth Chatto, Rosemary Verey, Christopher Lloyd, Penelope Hobhouse and Ann Lovejoy, experimenting all the time with plant associations and plant placement.

"Getting cancer ten years ago was the turning point for me and the garden. I had to stop working, I don't drive and I couldn't dig. So, I was forced to sit in my own garden and look." With an idea from her friend Wally Bishop she moved all the hot, dry plants in bright pinks, mauves and reds to the front garden's southern exposure. The wetter plants in oranges and yellows with golden and bronze foliage were moved to the damp, back garden.

"I began to see the back garden as a series of islands with rivers of lawn flowing in between. The back garden used to be a bog and I got fed up fighting the damp alkaline soil. Now I go with it." Elizabeth has benches tucked away in both the front and back gardens for resting and private viewing. "The garden has been a great psychological boost. It is cheerful to sit among colours you love. Foliage lasts so much longer than flowers."

From the back steps of the England residence are pots of tender plants such as *Lavandula stoechas*, purple osteospermum, rosemary, variegated iris, sedums, and sempervivums. Your eye follows a curved path containing lady's-mantle, arctic willow, and purple sage growing in the foreground. A variegated kerria, *Euphorbia characias*, and yellow daylilies are planted behind to provide foliage cover for the golden rambling rose 'Alister Stella Gray,' a noisette, a deep red *Rosa moyesii* 'Geranium,' and the delicately scented climber 'Golden Wings.' The very tall grass *Stipa gigantea* shivered in the wind, catching the afternoon light.

At the head of the curve was a striking yellow bamboo behind golden *Kniphofia* 'Queen of the Prairie' with *Penstemon utahensis*, *Centaurea macrocephala*, and a highly scented, yellow-flowering jasmine. In the opposite border Elizabeth contrasts the iridescent *Filipendula ulmaria* 'Aurea' with a drift of glossy evergreen groundcover and a backdrop of large-leafed hostas. The garden glows with the golden foliage accents. Deep red Japanese maples and bronze heuchera are planted throughout for contrast.

In the centre of the back "islands" is a corkscrew willow beside pots of lilies. The fragrant hybrid martagon lilies do well in shady, alkaline conditions. Another salt lover is the unusual, yellow-flowered, blue-green leafed shrub *Bupleurum fruticosum* which Elizabeth obtained from Christopher Lloyd in England. When Penelope Hobhouse visited the garden, she noticed it right away and declared the shrub to be her favourite.

In a shady back corner is another English import, the heavily scented David Austen rose 'Golden Celebration' surrounded by *Geranium macrorrhizum* 'Album,' *Euphorbia griffithii* 'Fireglow,' and *Clematis montana* 'Marjorie' among self-seeded apricot-coloured foxgloves. The garden is packed with unusual plant material. A visiting student was surprised when Elizabeth's garden was on a rose tour. The student could not see any roses. "Actually, I have thirty-seven different varieties," laughed Elizabeth. "They are all in there." Her favourite is the silky-yellow tea rose 'Lady Hillingdon,' which smells of tea and produces reddish-purple young leaves.

The front garden is equally packed with unusual plants in more romantic tones of blue, mauve and pink. In the shade of the afternoon, my eye was caught by *Filipendula camtschatica* with purple stems, a deep-blue bearded iris, and the purple globes of *Allium christophii* in front of the pink Bourbon rose 'Zépherine Drouhin.' It is the kind of garden you could return to again and

In the sunny front yard, Elizabeth removed all the grass, dumped gravel and planted a blaze of perennial colour that could withstand the hot, dry conditions. Her neighbours were not amused.

again and still miss some new gem that Elizabeth has collected.

A dedicated member of the Victoria Horticultural Society's Hardy Plant Group, Elizabeth said of her association, "Before I joined, I gardened in isolation and had no one with whom to share ideas and successes. I've learned so much from the Hardy Plant Group." She grows many plants by seed and shares plants with group members. "The group is a great place to ask questions and talk endlessly about a particular plant or plant design, without people thinking you are crazy."

Unfortunately, Elizabeth's neighbours have not always shared her sense of style. When she removed all the lawn in the front and dumped gravel

for her hot, dry perennials, neighbours complained to the municipality about the "eyesore." They were informed that Mrs. England's garden was just featured on the local television gardening show with Doris Page and on David Tarrant's gardening program in Vancouver. "That shut them up," Elizabeth recalled, laughing. "Other people walk by and say, 'What a jungle.'"

Elizabeth was definitely ahead of her time with her emphasis on foliage. Now people come from all over the world to see her work. "It is very important to show your garden, especially to young people. I guess it is the librarian and educator in me. I want to reach people with what I do because they are the future."

Happy Valley Herb Farm
The Garden of Lynda & Michael Dowling

The lavender harvest begins early in the morning at Happy Valley Herb Farm, a labour of love for Linda and Michael Dowling.

ynda and Michael Dowling live in Langford on property settled by Lynda's grandparents in 1910. The Dowlings cleared the land of broom, brambles, wild grasses, and rose thickets by having work bees. "We bribed our friends with chocolate cake," laughed Lynda. Finally after two years of intense garden preparation they moved a trailer to the site, and later, in 1986, the whole family.

At first the herb garden was a small demonstration area beside the chicken shed and a rockery. Nine years later, the herb farm encom-

The butterfly garden at Happy Valley Herb Farm with poppies, valerian, clarkia, lovage, fennel, borage and a border of oregano and chives.

passes most of their three acres with enormous fields of lavender. One field is solid blue-mauve *Lavandula angustifolia* 'Munstead' from cuttings the Dowlings made seven years ago. The second field contains successive rows of traditional blue *Lavandula spica*; deep purple *Lavandula angustifolia* 'Hidcote,' which Lynda grew from seed sent by her mother-in-law in England; and pale mauve *Lavandula vera* whose seed Noel Richardson from Ravenhill Herb Farm brought to Lynda from France. They also have one row of pale pink *Lavandula rosea*. Every year, they harvest the lavender in a big work bee. Last year, their fifth year of production, a thousand plants produced eighty-three pounds of dried lavender, the bulk of which went to Butchart Gardens for resale while a small portion went to local florists. It is a splendid site to see the lavender fields ripple in the summer breeze, giving off their heady scent.

The original plan was for Happy Valley Herb Farm to be a job for Lynda while raising her children. The Dowlings wanted to produce plant material for local people. They credit retired plantsman Murray Cooke, from Sooke, with much of their early inspiration and support. They knew they needed a display garden but it was more years of work amid rearing young children before the land was totally cleared for planting. The Dowlings put in an eight-foot-high deer fence and planted more fruit trees in the existing King apple orchard. They added plantings of rhubarb, blackberries, gooseberries, and raspberries while saving seeds from poppies, cowslips, and columbine they found in the fields. The cedar hedge, planted by Lynda's grandparents, provides privacy from the road and is an excellent wind break. Compost and truckloads of cow manure are added to the soil every season.

Happy Valley Herb Farm is a true organic farm. "My grandfather didn't use anything but dynamite for stumps," mused Lynda. "We are committed to growing plants without spraying." The Dowlings supply the Empress Hotel and several restaurants in Victoria with fresh-cut herbs and edible flowers such as daylilies, *Rosa rubifolia*, gentian sage, tuberous begonias, honeysuckle, calendula, Johnny

jump-ups, and borage flowers. They supply dried flowers to shops and Lynda teaches herb classes at the Juan de Fuca Recreation Centre, Camosun College, and the Royal B.C. Museum, as well as two classes at the farm. In July the class is on edible flowers and, in August, on women and herbs. "We make flower tiaras under the apple tree," Lynda explained. Michael Dowling works full-time in Victoria as a landscaper but the family puts in many hours on weekends and in the evenings maintaining the farm. They have future plans of turning the old shed into a teahouse overlooking the display garden.

The garden is trellised with the dense bush rose *Rosa rugosa* 'Roseraie de L'Hay,' which blooms from late May to July. Within the trellis is a wheelchair-accessible formal planting with clipped germander borders separating four beds of herbs planted for landscaping, culinary, medicinal, and craft uses. In the centre is an obelisk on a raised platform with creeping thyme surrounded by small beds of sweet william, pansies, and *Verbena bonariensis*. The landscaping bed has Jerusalem sage, white mullein (*Verbascum chaixii* 'Album'), lamb's ears, and tall yellow verbascum in the background. In the foreground is *Artemisia absinthium* 'Lambrook Silver,' *A. versicolor*, *Santolina rosmarinifolia*, with borage, nigella, and white nicotiana that is self-seeding.

The culinary bed is composed of purple sage, sorrel, golden oregano, yellow daylilies, calendula, scented geranium 'Mabel Grey,' blue gentian sage, tarragon, bronze fennel, rosemary, chives, and bay. The medicinal garden is full of rampant chamomile with foxgloves, valerian, and purple *Echinacea purpurea* in the background. A yellow 'Fru Dagmar Hastrup' rose dominates the craft garden along with a border of deep-purple lavender, while Clary sage, astrantia, scented geraniums, and poppies compete for space. It is a well maintained garden with the casual touch of plants that are self-seeding. The Dowlings are avid seed collectors and sowers. Customers leave their address if they want seeds for the next year.

The butterfly garden is an example of growing plants from seed. Lynda sowed several flats of asclepius two years ago and found rare monarch

The vigorous Rosa rugosa *'Roseraie de L'Hay' surrounds the trellised garden which is wheelchair accessible.*

butterflies laying eggs. Twenty-four monarchs were successfully released and, although they have not returned to date, Lynda has planted a whole garden of valerian, clarkia, dianthus, lovage, fennel, borage, chives, and oregano around a buddleia to encourage their return. She is a member of the Butterfly Club and encourages other gardeners to plant gardens for butterflies. Swallowtails have laid egg cases throughout the herb garden, even on the walls of the greenhouse where the Dowlings raise their plants. They are constantly adding to and experimenting with culinary plants. They cultivate alpine strawberries in red, pink, and white forms. Very tender herbs, such as *Lavandula stoechas* in pale pink and yellow, grow in their protected "dry house."

The Dowlings' business has expanded. Now they hire people to help with propagation and maintenance as it is a full-time job just keeping track of the public requests for garden visits and speaking engagements, but Lynda and Michael are tireless workers. They continue to expand the garden, trading plants with other gardeners while constantly planting and seed collecting. They look forward to the garden maturing just as they marvel at the speed at which their children are growing. Next year, their daughter will start school and, as Lynda said, "Now our son won't be the only student with peanut butter and rose petal jelly sandwiches."

The Garden of Mary Henderson

A *white jasmine vine encircles Diascia, the white rose 'Alba maxima,' purple salpiglossis and yellow lily 'Amber Gold' in a planting of "controlled chaos" beside Mary Henderson's outdoor swimming pool.*

Mary Henderson has lived in the same house for over forty-two years. The large, nearly two-acre waterfront property located in Gordon Head has changed during that time. But more so in the last four years as Mary began to focus full-time on the garden.

When the Hendersons and their three children moved to the property in the early '50s, the garden was surrounded by enormous arbutus trees shading the house and dropping leaves on a rockery originally planted by alpine expert Ed Lohbrunner. There was a wide, formal hybrid tea-rose terrace by the sea surrounded by a clipped *Lonicera nitida* hedge and the entire property was rimmed by Monterey cypress (*Cupressus macrocarpa*).

A bitterly cold winter in 1955 severely damaged the *Lonicera* hedge and killed the cypresses. Two of the arbutus succumbed to disease. A swimming pool was built in the '60s for the teenage children. In the early '70s the Hendersons hired Vancouver landscape architects Philip Tattersfield

and Bob Punderson, who designed a courtyard sheltered from the wind, and a sandstone patio to replace the old lawn on the windward seaview side. A large central sloping lawn with curved outline replaced the triple terracing over the expanse of property separating house from sea. They moved all the shrubs to the borders of the property for what they thought to be a low-maintenance garden. Bob Lang was in charge of the landscaping maintenance and old photos attest to Bob's skill with bulbs, annuals, and potted plants. It wasn't until the late 1980s when Mary, now retired and widowed with children grown, had time to devote to her garden. One of her first acts was to put out a call for help.

A local gardening authority, Doris Page, suggested soil expert and plantsman Jim Hofmann, and Mary gives Jim all the credit for the existing beauty. Mary works every day in the garden, all year long, involving herself in as much of the garden development and maintenance as she is able.

Here we find perennials that can withstand the sun and wind and not impede the ocean front view, such as Dictamus albus, *foxgloves,* Rosa 'Ballerina,' *deep-red* Centranthus ruber, *and blue* Veronica spicata incana.

She now admits, "This is not a low maintenance garden." Blayne Asmundson maintains the garden three days a week but it is Mary and Jim that are ambitiously finding (seed lists, catalogues, friends, etc.), propagating (grown from seed, cuttings, etc.), and gardening the burgeoning number of plant species and cultivars in the garden. Recently, mixed wetland borders, alpine and rock gardens, wall gardens, a cool Mediterranean seaside garden, a bog garden, and elaborate container gardening schemes have been the focus of their garden development.

Each landscape has its own set of planting limitations and problems presented by the site, climate, and exposure to wind. "The soils on the higher elevations are sandy loam over gravel," explained Jim. Consequently, drainage is not a problem except at the mid elevation where clay was used to build the old rose terrace now covered over by grass. That created bog-like conditions in the sloping lawn which had to be repaired. Underground water discharges from the surrounding land drains through the Henderson's garden and invasive plant material such as bindweed, blackberries, horsetail, and maple seedlings from the neighbouring "wild" properties are a constant challenge. "Finessing the garden," said Jim, "has been dealing with all of these problems."

The day I visited, Mary was working in the house while Blayne watered all the potted seedlings, which number in the thousands and occupy both the cold and warm greenhouses, cold frames, decks, stairs, and patios. All the pots are labelled and inventoried in a computer system by family, genus, bloom colour, bloom season, growing conditions, pest susceptibility, etc. Mary spends winter nights on her grand-daughter's computer to make the lists, using the "Garden Encyclopedia and Maintenance Program" that was co-designed by Jim and a computer science student and landscaper named Warren Kennedy.

We sat on the sandstone terrace overlooking the vast grounds and sea beyond. An eye-catching planting extending into the terrace was dominated by the silk tree *Albizia julibrissin* 'Rosea,' which was braced against the prevailing wind; the underplanting consisted of *Potentilla nepalensis*

with *Nepeta* x *faassenii*, *Lavatera* 'Burgundy Wine,' *Eryngium amethystinum*, *Oenothera missouriensis*, *Salvia* x *superba*, *Echinops ritro*, *Santolina rosmarinifolia*, *S. chamaecyparissus*, *Helianthemum* 'Ben Aflek,' *Pennisetum villosum*, *Lonicera nitida* 'Baggesen's Gold,' and martagon lilies looking down at the open faces of the dwarf Shasta daisies. The bed provides colour from early spring to late fall.

"You have to use bright colours in the full sun," Jim explained when I asked him about colour selection. He pointed to another corner planting with *Euphorbia amygdaloides* subsp. *robbiae*, the tender *Podocarpus macrophyllus*, yellow *Lonicera* 'Baggesen's Gold' with *Geranium* 'Johnson's Blue,' *Rosa* 'Royal Bassano,' and the show stopper *Aquilegia vulgaris*. "The sea-coast light intensity competes with pale colours and washes them out. With the sun, and the glare from the water, intense colours and foliage contrasts are essential."

In the cracks of the patio Jim has added over twenty-six genera with eleven different varieties of thyme, including the heavily scented *Thymus serphyllum* (Raspberry Ripple) and the low grey woolly *Thymus* 'Vey' in the heavy traffic areas. Deep purple *Calendrinia umbellata* (Amaranth) with *Acaena* 'Blue Haze' and pink *Geranium orientalitibeticum*, *G. sanguineum*, *G. sessililforum* are in contrast to grey convolvulus, hyssop, and silver *Veronica spicata incana*.

Walking down the lawn and facing the terrace Jim built granite dry walls for full sun and exposure terracing with perennials that can withstand the wind and not impede the view. The planting emphasizes continual changes, with pale pink moss rose 'Ballerina,' blue *Anchusa* 'Feltham Pride,' *Dictamus albus*, blue-purple *Perovskia atriplicifolia*, *Aster novae-angliae* 'Alma Potschke,' *Crocosmia solfataire* and many species of hardy geranium, to name just a few species in this complex planting.

Jim has built gravel paths through the large tree and shrub perimeters all the way to the sea. The soil is terraced for planting, building drainage ditches which act as stream beds with rustic wooden bridges. Rivers of primulas seeded by Mary are planted in the wet sites, including the tender *Primula polyneura*. Perennials and shrubs are grown in

Jim Hoffman and Mary Henderson have planted over twenty-six genera with eleven different species of thyme in the cracks of the slate terrace.

mass plantings for impact in the shade of weeping birches, old fruit trees and enormous conifers.

Mary has donated the sea frontage to Saanich, and botanists Adolf and Aluna Ceska are saving seeds of native plants to re-establish the indigenous flora in the exposed site. Jim has established *Rosa virginiana*, grown from seed, along the seaside fence because of its scent and wind resistance. The plan for this area is a cool Mediterranean garden with *Photinia serrulata*, yucca, ficus, shrubby *Alyssums*, grasses, and small native bulbs.

Up at the house Mary showed me her alpine rockery, which she can see out of her kitchen window. "It is one of the few areas in a big garden where she can appreciate small plants." said Jim. There are over two hundred alpine species and cultivars bordered by Italian broom, yew and Chinese photinia. Jim has great plans for a rockery at the entrance of the property. He pointed out many unusual potted plants placed strategically in every corner, with great care given to foliage contrast and continuous interest.

"This garden is about controlled chaos," said Jim enthusiastically. "There must be exuberance and interesting plants everywhere."

The Garden of Mr. and Mrs. Stuart Holland

*M*rs. Holland leaves the gate open to her garden every spring. Planted by her late husband, the garden is full of mature hybrid rhododendrons.

Stuart Holland designed his garden on Transit Road in Oak Bay so that there would be beautiful blossoms in the spring and colourful foliage in the fall. As the chief geologist for the province, and author of the definitive geological reference text *Landforms of British Columbia*, he was away in the field for much of the summer; consequently, summer colour did not interest him. But every spring in April and May the gate at the Holland home is left open for visitors to share the beauty of more than four hundred rhododendrons and azaleas in bloom.

Mr. Holland's interest in plants began when he was working in the mountains of northern B.C. With a simple field guide he began to identify what he saw. Back home in Victoria during a chance walk through Beacon Hill park in winter, Mr. Holland saw snow-capped blooming rhododendrons that piqued his interest. He began to search out plants and was indeed "hooked on rhododendrons."

In the early '50s he bought plants from the nursery of Ted and Mary Greig at Royston. He also started growing rhododendrons from seed obtained from The Royal Horticultural Society in England, the Edinburgh Botanical Garden, and from a seed collector in Darjeeling, India. Mr. Holland and his wife Diana bought their Oak Bay property and replaced the war-time Victory Garden with trees: birch, crabapple, flowering cherry, magnolia, and arbutus to provide shade and wind protection for the fledgling rhododendrons.

As a scientist, Mr. Holland kept scrupulous records of temperature and moisture conditions. The garden naturally slopes westward so that drainage is excellent. Mr. Holland watered heavily in the late spring and early summer when the rhododendrons were making their new top growth but after July he reduced watering to a minimum. He never fertilized his plants but mulched heavily with leaves and coarse peat moss. With time he established over three hundred rhododendrons comprising two hundred species and

A late spring rhododendron reaches for the sun in Mrs. Holland's crowded garden, now a forest of hybrid rhododendrons.

hybrids. He even established his own hybrids, the most famous being 'Transit Gold' (a cross between Greig's 'Royal Flush' and Ludlow and Sherriff's *xanthocodon* 17521), with a lovely, large, golden yellow blossom. In 1986 he was awarded the American Rhododendron Society Bronze medal, the highest award given, in recognition of his expertise.

The Holland garden today is a forest of rhododendrons. The long narrow lot is packed with mature plants that compete with each other for sunlight and moisture. Well-planned brick paths meander throughout the garden for easy viewing. The rhododendrons are underplanted with hellebores, anemones, oxalis, and native lilies and ferns. From the house there is a "picture" in every window.

The garden slopes away from the house, so that the viewer has the advantage of looking down on the blossom-laden shrubs. While walking down the brick paths you must look up to see the blooms that give the whole garden an intimate woodland appeal. Azaleas mingle with rhododendrons. As one shrub finishes another explodes with colour and the paths become strewn with faded blossoms.

Mr. Holland was not content with just this garden. He helped grow rooted cuttings for the rhododendrons at Playfair Park in Saanich. An executive member of the Victoria Rhododendron Society, the Rock and Alpine Club, and the Thetis Park Nature Sanctuary Association, he was also appointed a member of the University Garden Friends and helped establish the acclaimed rhododendron gardens at the University of Victoria from the Buchanon-Simpson garden at Cowichan Lake. Mr. Holland was always one to share his knowledge and plants. Cuttings and seeds of his hybridizing experiments are now growing in gardens throughout Victoria and the Saanich Peninsula, both public and private. His final written work, co-written with Brian Dale, was a history of the pioneer Ucluelet nurseryman, George Fraser.

Today, Mrs. Elizabeth Holland maintains the garden with the help of gardener Jim Ahlers, as a living memorial to her husband who died in March, 1989, just as the garden was coming into bloom.

In the early spring, the soft pink camellia variety 'Mary Christian' blooms by a garden gate, while hellebores and primroses flower beneath.

The Garden of Robin Hopper and Judi Dyelle

The garden of Robin Hopper and Judi Dyelle has strong oriental influences.

Robin Hopper is known for his award-winning pottery. The first recipient in Canada of the prestigious Bronfman Award for Excellence, Robin has an eye for form. Now, he and his wife, Judi Dyelle, are gaining a reputation for their stunning Metchosin garden.

Mature Douglas fir trees shade the front entrance where Robin cleared the underbrush of snowberry, blackberries, and brambles. He moved into his semi-derelict heritage house in 1977 and spent a year renovating before tackling the garden. Because of the size of the six-acre property, Robin wanted large mature shrubs. He exchanged his hand-made pots for truckloads of mature rhododendrons from experts Stuart Holland and Albert de Mezey; included was Mr. Holland's prize rhodo, 'Transit Gold.' It is growing well by the front door while *Rhododendron fulvum* and *R. fictolacteum*, both huge specimens, are on the west side of the house.

By 1978 Robin built a lily pond off the back deck. In the early spring *Magnolia stellata* is splendid, in company with azaleas, candelabra primulas, and a Japanese cherry tree. In the summer Japanese iris, both purple and pale mauve, stand out against the weeping larch, horizontal junipers, and Japanese maples. Robin made a point of choosing drooping and weeping stock to reinforce the "waterfall" motif. The curved form is replicated by the plant material, which provides interest in every season.

Shady areas around the water are ideal spots for rushes, hostas, and *Iris ensata* and *I. sibirica*. In the centre of the pond is a small fountain that oxygenates the water for the resident koi and goldfish. Two replica eighteenth-century Thai bronze herons were recently added but indigenous great blue herons have been observed eating goldfish.

Thai bronze herons are the focal point in the koi-studded pond in front of the brilliant Japanese maple, Acer palmatum 'Osakazuki.'

Consequently, netting has become a necessary evil to protect the fish.

Another pool was added four years later, complete with a Japanese waterspout. Robin describes this planting as his pink and white garden. *Actinidia kolomikta* clings to the house behind salmon pink azaleas 'Davisii,' apple-blossom-coloured *Rhododendron yakushimanum*, *Magnolia grandiflora*, *Pieris japonica* 'Variegata,' and *Macleaya cordata* (plume poppy) with spikes of pink flowers and lobed grey-green foliage. In the summer, lady's-mantle billows over the border and *Clematis macropetala* is an excellent contrast to the pink and white foliage of the actinidia.

The deck, once covered in a pergola of wisteria that died one severe winter, has recently been rebuilt to incorporate a herb garden, which is easily accessible from the kitchen. Tarragon, rosemary, marjoram, oregano, sage, and savory are planted in raised beds for easy picking. The white grape 'Himrod' grows on the trellis now, and Robin would like to add more vines but Judi prefers the bare lines of the wood.

Robin describes the garden as Anglo-Japanadian. Because he and Judi travel internationally to Japan, China, and Thailand, oriental influences are strong but they are careful to use local rock and incorporate native plant material.

Robin is building woodland walks on the west side of the property with plants obtained from the Victoria Horticultural Society and the Hardy Plant Group (they are members). Under the shade of a plum tree are hostas, foxgloves, ferns, meadow rue, primulas, epimedium, calla lilies, and ivy—all in white. Stepping stones placed carefully in moss lead the viewer through the woodland retreat to an opening with the enormous leaves of *Rodgersia podophylla*, the late-flowering rhododendron 'Polar Bear' and the unusual heart-shaped foliage of the katsura tree, *Cercidiphyllum japonicum*.

The path leads to the front of the house where large cotoneasters and viburnums (*V.* x *juddii*, *V. plicatum*), obtained from demolition sales, thrive. By the front door is *Cornus florida*, maidenhair ferns, and a vine hydrangea growing against the house. In a dry bed opposite, Robin has used pale granite rock and stones as an understorey to Rhododendron augustinii and *R. calophytum*. It is sculptural but blends in with the native landscape.

Trees, shrubs, and grasses are used as sculptural accents throughout this garden. Beyond the potting shed is the dramatic, pendulous golden cedar (*Cedrus deodara* 'Aurea') and the unusual golden raintree (*Koelreuteria paniculata*) with yellow flowers in July and beautiful seed pods. Towards the storage barn a bamboo grove in a moist shady spot is a statement on foliage contrast: it contains golden bamboo (*Phyllostachys aureosulcata*), black bamboo (*P. nigra*), timber bamboo (*P. bambusoides*), kuma bamboo (*Sasa veitchii*), and arrow bamboo (*Pseudosasa japonica*) beside Japanese bloodgrass. There is ample space for this planting to grow without fear of encroachment from other plants.

The soil is so good that Robin rarely adds anything to it. There is one-and-a-half feet of topsoil over clay. They do have help with lawn mowing and spring and fall cleanup. Watering is a major commitment but Robin and Judi keep at it and hope to drill a well in the southern end of the property for the garden.

Beyond the orchard of pears, apples, plums, and crabapples is a hot, grey bed with cardoons, fennel, sweet cicely, grey salvia, and large, grey Scotch thistle (*Onopordum acanthium*) with the climbing rose 'Blanc Double de Coubert' growing thirty feet up into a hawthorn tree and joining a *Wisteria venusta* coming from the other side. A huge Japanese umbrella plant (*Petasites japonicus*) and a yellow tree peony (*Paeonia lutea*) grow in a bed with rhododendrons 'Lotus White,' 'Goldsworth Yellow,' and 'Virginia Richards.'

Robin and Judi have built a new one-of-a-kind gallery off their old showroom for the sale of new work, books, and videos. The landscaping around the new Japanese-inspired building is in the form of a Japanese walled courtyard garden. The outside of the wall will become home to espaliered figs and peach trees. Help from pool expert and garden designer Michael Greenfield includes a new koi pool, teahouse, and low Chinese-style bridge crossing the narrows between existing and new pools. "It started out as a two-month project," explained Robin, "Now it has been two years. We just

A water spout pours into a small pond in a pink and white planting of Actinidia kolomikta, Pieris japonica *'Variegata'* *and* Macleaya cordata.

have to sell more pots."

Robin and Judi leave for a workshop-teaching tour of Australia in the early spring to teach new and old concepts in pottery making. As much as they love travelling, they proudly enjoy the ambience of their home and garden in Metchosin as well as the quality of life that Victoria has to offer.

The Johnson Garden

The Johnson garden has something to offer even in January. Pink heather accents the rockery in front of the Chinese teahouse. The terra-cotta pots are from Italy.

Most of us buy properties with houses and gardens designed by someone else. We inherit the bones of someone else's garden and slowly, over time, make our mark. If we are lucky, the original house and garden were designed together and so our changes are merely cosmetic; but if we are not lucky, more drastic changes may be necessary.

The Johnson garden is one of the lucky ones where the house was designed around an existing garden. That garden was planted ninety years ago. What remains of this original Edwardian planting is surprising and restores my faith in planting trees no matter how slow growing they may be.

This original Maclure house sits on a height of land amid two-and-a-half acres in the heart of Oak Bay. It was built behind granite walls at a time when families were large and the number of staff even larger. Estates grew their own vegetables and fruits and large areas of property were devoted to amusements. You can imagine puffy-sleeved ladies playing croquet and straw-hatted gentlemen batting tennis balls. The property boasted a Chinese-style tennis house in which to observe the goings-on.

During the Depression, pressures from ill health forced the owners to subdivide the property and a house was constructed in the old orchard beside the walnut tree and golden plum. The Maclure house was subsequently bought by a retired couple from England, Alfred and Marjorie Johnson. They lived there until the mid-'40s, whereupon they moved to the smaller house in the orchard. They decided to take the Chinese-style tennis house with them and moved it down the hill on logs. The Johnsons were consummate gardeners with an eye for symmetry and design. They planted a garden in the 1940s that remains today as one of the finest in Victoria.

Old photos from the post-war years show the Johnsons' new home as a dark house shrouded by firs and laurels. The Johnsons cut down the suffo-

Calla lilies show up splendidly against the dark green foliage of this partially shaded border.

49

cating shrubs to let in the light. They removed a solid wood enclosure in the front and replaced it with a trellised fence and gate. Mr. Johnson wound Chinese wisteria and clematis throughout the trellis for a succession of blooms from spring to fall.

In the backyard, the Johnsons filled in an old pond in the middle of the lawn and expanded the natural pools in the exposed bedrock adjacent to the Chinese pagoda, now used as a teahouse. Stone steps leading to the old tennis court remain but a row of filbert trees (Kentish cobs) were planted for privacy and for the delicious nuts. Mr. Johnson tore down the narrow brick wall of the patio, doubled its size and laid pale blue Virginia slate. The house is now painted a matching pale blue. Rhododendrons and azaleas were introduced as a colourful spring background for all the borders. Watering was never a problem because the Johnsons put in one of the first underground watering systems in the 1950s.

They grew many of the flowers for the garden from seed in the greenhouse. Mrs. Johnson grew delphiniums, annuals, and even tuberous begonias from seed (sprouted on bricks) to plant in the garden after the spring bulbs had died back. Mrs. Johnson worked in the garden for thirty-five years until 1981. She willed the Chinese teahouse to her granddaughter, Sarah, but as no one was able to move it, the teahouse remains as a permanent fixture on the property.

The garden was abandoned for seven years during a succession of real estate deals, which further subdivided the side vegetable lot and top section without touching the main garden. Then the present owner, who was being forced to leave her very large house and acreage, saw the Johnson garden by chance over the stone wall.

"It was love at first sight. I could see the bones of a beautiful garden and so I turned to the realtor and said, 'I'll take it.' The realtor replied, 'Don't you want to see the house?'"

The present owner brought a few camellias and irises from her old garden and added hostas in shady places. Her large Italian terra-cotta pots were placed strategically but the original garden remains intact. From the slate patio the garden rises like an amphitheatre, totally private, with seasonal colour throughout. You can see part of the garden from every room in the house. It is a lasting testament to the original Maclure house and to the Johnsons' subsequent garden design. The owners may change but the bones of this garden will carry on into the next century.

A stunning perennial border in the Johnson garden. The present owner has added spring bulbs, iris, hostas, heathers and forget-me-nots to the existing planting of rhododendrons, azaleas and Japanese maple.

The Garden of Karen Jones

A worn wicker chair and a bloom-laden rose set the tone for this well-planned tangle. In the foreground are old roses 'Belle Isis' and 'Souvenir d'Alphonse Lavallée'.

Karen Jones had a vision of an English country garden, the kind she read about in turn-of-the-century books. Twenty-two years later she has such a garden which she planned, ripped out, replanted, moved, replanted and finally, after twenty-two years, has left as is. "I did have a plan," she said. "Of course, if I had stuck to it, my garden would have been done years ago but I changed my mind every year. It is only in the last few years that the garden has basically stayed put.

"When I moved here, the garden had raised mounds in every corner. I flattened the front and built the back into three levels, sloping away from the house. In the process I dug up hundreds and hundreds of boulders which I used to border the beds. The smaller rocks became the gravel on which I poured a thin layer of concrete for the paths. I ripped out the grass—everything but the Garry oak trees. It took me ten years. By this time I had discovered old roses and was aiming for a natural, overgrown look."

Karen, a single, working mother who makes her own slipcovers, curtains, and clothes (for herself and her Victorian dolls), does not have a great deal of time to weed, water, stake, or tidy up. As a result, the garden is mulched with municipal leaf mulch, a foot thick in places to prevent desiccation and to cut down on weeding. "Because of the mulch I can't have tiny, tiddly plants. The borders are self-maintaining. I clean up twice a year, and I try to water two hours a week. In between, I don't have time," said Karen.

The day I visited, Karen's dining room table was covered in a rose chintz tablecloth. In the centre was a gold-rimmed bowl in which floated

In the foreground, the blood red rose 'Tuscany Superb' is glorious beside the blue spires of delphinium. Nigella, dianthus and perennial geraniums seed freeely among the flagstones.

sweet-scented roses. There were deep pink Damask 'Ispahan,' pale pink 'Celsiana,' deep-red gallica 'Tuscany Superb,' pale blush 'Grüssan Aachen' and the hybrid perpetual 'Souvenir d'Alphonse Lavallée.' "I like this method of cutting," said Karen, "because you don't have to remove half the plant to find one blossom." Most of her roses came from Pickering in Ontario. She is a member of the Old Rose Group and, like her colleagues, does not drive, loves cats (Karen has four), and is a collector. Lately, however, she admits to having reached her limit with exotic plants. "Every time I get something weird and wonderful I end up having to get rid of it. I think I am past needing to have everything."

Looking out the leaded glass window of the sitting room you can see a border that provides colour for ten months of the year. Beginning with hellebores in January, then spring bulbs with perennial forget-me-nots, leading to the summer and many roses: 'Belle de Crècy,' 'Duchesse de Montebello,' 'Souvenir d'Alphonse Lavallée,' 'Charles de Mills.' There are also six different climbing clematis, among them 'Duchess of Edinburgh' and the vigorous 'Huldine.' In the late summer Japanese anemones flower and, when the colder weather begins, rose hips are formed as the leaves begin to yellow. "It is a satisfying border," said Karen, who uses branches from an old pear tree to prop up the bloom-laden roses. "It is important not to let the prop cancel out the casualness of the rose," she explained.

On the other side of this border my eye was drawn to a shed under an akebia vine where Karen keeps her worn wicker chairs. "I made the shed and all the trellises from old packing cases," she said. The border begins with the unusual *Kirengeshoma palmata*, a shade-loving plant that produces cream-coloured flowers in late summer. Beside it are the yellow self-seeded corydalis, hardy geraniums in deep purple and pale pink, royal blue delphinium, pale purple *Viola cornuta*, and blue and mauve tradescantia.

In the centre bed amid stepping stones is a yellow and pink oenothera, pale blue nigella, pink poppies, blue and white campanula, lychnis, plum astrantia, white canterbury bells, tall coral penstemon, and an orange-pink rock rose. "I used to separate out colours but, after a while, I found it too monotonous. I think you need yellow and orange for contrast. Now I prefer a jumble of colours," Karen explained. Yet she admitted that a tiny corner—with silver artemisia 'Huntington,' blue-green leafed valerian, self-seeded sweet rocket tucked in behind a wooden bench—all worked beautifully because of the blending of the soft colours and foliage.

On the side garden, Karen plants an extensive range of vegetables and fruits with a "holding area" for plants in transition. Against the house under the eaves where it is dry are spectacular "waterlily" dahlias in peach tones beside the scented tea rose, *Rosa sombreuil*, climbing up the wall. By the front trellis is the impressive pink-scented climbing rose, 'Constance Spry.'

The front garden is full of colour. Within the lavender lilac there is a blooming clematis, along with the roses 'Prosperity' and 'Pompom Blanc Parfait'; a nearby border consists of a very fragrant mock orange, sweet rocket, and the myrrh-scented rose 'Belle Amour,' Karen's favourite. In the foreground is valerian, Japanese anemones, and golden phlomis following a drift of spring tulips, among them the dramatic black 'Queen of Night.' The plants spill out onto the path in a well-planned tangle.

Karen has help periodically from landscape consultant Neil Knowlton, who understands her need for a natural cottage garden but sometimes disagrees with what is natural and what is a tangle. She and Neil have been discussing changes to the bed by the front steps where Karen wants a drift of groundcover while Neil would prefer a more specific planting. By the front door an old wicker chair has variegated ivy for a seat, surrounded by pots with annuals and climbers.

As I was leaving, Karen talked about another vision she had of cementing all her broken antique blue and white china into a path or pool in the back corner. She has an uncanny ability to put together ordinary things in extraordinary ways.

An ivy-covered wicker chair on the front porch.

The Garden of Elizabeth Kerfoot

Elizabeth Kerfoot uses her painterly eye to blend colours in the garden. In this summer planting are the tall green flowers of Nicotiana alata *'Limestone Green,' pink N. 'Nicki Series',* Hosta halcyon, *pink begonias, white impatiens and in the background pale pink* Lavatera *'Barnsley.'*

*E*lizabeth Kerfoot observes the season's colours in her garden from her kitchen window, her sunroom, and her studio. These observations are the basis for her masterful paintings—landscapes predominate, but even her fine portraits include flowers and foliage, aspects of the garden.

Gardening was in her blood when, as a child of four, she remembers planting seeds in the large vegetable garden. Raised on the North Saanich property "up the hill," Elizabeth never imagined she would end up living in the vegetable patch. But fourteen years ago, she and her husband built a house on seven-and-a-half acres and are still finishing off the details, bartering paintings for trellis work and stone masonry. One acre is under cultivation with an enormous vegetable and cutting garden. One half-acre is planted in blueberries as a cash crop, two acres are hay fields and the remaining land is left wild with a pond and a forest of alders, firs and cedars.

"We really feel the seasons here," said Elizabeth. "There is an east-west breeze but we are in a slight hollow sheltering us from the southwesterly gales that hit Victoria." Archaeologists speculate the site was once a prehistoric winter campsite for aboriginals, chosen because of its protection. In her great uncle's and parents' time, cattle were raised and the pond was made by excavating peat soil.

When I arrived to view the garden, Elizabeth was selling the last of the day's blueberry pickings. With two children at home, one taking home schooling, Elizabeth's days are full. Yet, she took time to show me a new west-facing, well-drained planting by the driveway. Against a hedge of *Rosa moyesii* 'Eddie's Crimson' was the exotic annual *Venidium* 'Zulu Prince' backed by various artemi-

*E*ven in the late fall there is something happening in the Kerfoot garden. Japanese anemones, meadow rue and hardy geraniums are a frothy backdrop for a worn chair and oak barrel water garden.

sias, grey-leafed *Helichrysum petiolare, Salvia* x *superba* 'Summer' with pink *Salvia superba*. There was also a *Viola tricolor* 'Bowles Black,' dark foliated dahlia 'Bishop of Llandoff' that Elizabeth predicted will be "clashing beautifully" beside the *Aster novae-angliae* 'Alma Potschke' with its brilliant pink petals and a rusty-orange eye. Yet to flower were violet cleomes, autumn sedums, and *Nicotiana sylvestris* which will tone down the "nervous duo."

As one of the designers of the renovated gardens at Government House, Elizabeth uses her painterly eye with colour and form. "What I like to see in public gardens is a variety of plants and design. All that bedding out is expensive and usually ho-hum. People are more sophisticated than given credit for. They want to see new ideas with plant groupings." For gardeners who feel intimidated by vast choices, she recommends Christopher Lloyd's books. "I like his colour courage and his creative solutions to keeping the garden attractive for most of the year."

Through her garden gate, by a small lawn and wooden bench, is a garden of soft tones. Pale salmon-coloured *Nicotiana* grow beside white *N. sylvestris*, and lime green *N. alata* blends with apricot-coloured tuberous begonias, and white impatiens; in the background are pale pink *Lavatera* 'Barnsley,' *Rosa* 'Empress Josephine,' the soft white of *Astrantia major*, spikes of *Acanthus spinosus*, grey-blue *Hosta* 'Halcyon,' and the arching purple bristles of fountain grass (*Pennisetum alopecuroides*). Under the shade of a Mt. Fuji Cherry tree are pink phlox, hardy geraniums, and astrantia, the latter seeding freely.

Elizabeth is a great seed collector and sower. She and her husband Pat are growing catalpa and paulownia trees from seed. She has exchanged seeds and cuttings with gardening friends of the Hardy Plant Study Group of the Victoria Horticultural Society and will be hosting the group in the fall in her garden. Each year, she and her husband spread at least three full loads of manure and compost: yards of rich organic matter that is spread two to four inches deep. "You must be as passionate about the soil as what is on top," Elizabeth explained. "And that means humus, humus and more humus!" She is a devout organic gardener

who waters by hand with warm, nutritious pond water. "The plants love it."

From her kitchen window, we sip tea staring out at the fruiting quince tree beside the brilliant *Robinia pseudoacacia* 'Frisia.' An understorey of *Lysimachia punctata*, feverfew, *Euonymus fortunei* 'Emerald and Gold' and numerous species of perennial geraniums surround a birdbath by stone stairs, in the shade of medlars and a blue Atlas cedar shrouded in *Clematis montana* var. *rubens*. Your eye is drawn down the path to the spectacular planting of cardoons in the vegetable garden beyond.

After our tea, we climbed over the deer fence to the pond. Ducks quacked, dragonflies (all fourteen different species) hummed, and butterflies darted about as we tramped through the peaty grassland. Elizabeth's parents once sold the peat to Butchart Gardens but today the pond is left as is, complete with bulrushes, water lilies, skunk cabbage, spearmint, peppermint, yellow monkeyflower, potentilla, the small-flowered bulrush (*Scirpus microcarpus*) with clusters of flowers, water plantain (*Alisma plantago-aquatica*), and a host of sedges. Elizabeth has added Japanese iris to the native flora and her magnolias and rhododendrons are doing well in the shady woodland. Her eldest daughter is building her own woodland walk in the forest where Elizabeth roamed as a child. Her younger daughter and friends have built a secret playhouse in the shrubs, weaving willow branches as walls with a container of blueberries in their "kitchen."

Walking back to the vegetable garden, we, too, stopped to munch succulent, sweet blueberries. The vegetable garden is complete with rows of beans, peas, purple sprouting broccoli, tomatoes, and salad greens. For cutting there are zinnias, lavatera, phygelius, and alstroemeria. "I love the surprises of gardening," declared Elizabeth, pointing to a mix of copper *Digitalis x mertonensis*, golden *Echinacea purpurea*, and rosy *Eupatorium purpureum* (Joe Pye weed). We passed the highly scented *Rosa* 'Constance Spry' and *R*. 'Shakespeare's Autumn Musk,' which will flower all summer. One of Elizabeth's favourite roses is *Rosa rugosa* 'Alba,' which produces beautiful hips in the summer and then blooms again in the fall.

On a rainy day in the cutting garden, perennial geraniums, sage, lamb's ears, campanula, the Damask moss rose 'William Lobb,' nigella and pink Peruvian lilies all work together beautifully.

The perennial borders were heavy with blossoms and flopped into the path. Deep burgundy species alstroemeria and blue *Campanula actiflora* flourished beside blue-purple *Buddleia nanhoensis*, entwined with the red-purple *Clematis viticella* 'Royal Velour.' Yellow nasturtiums, feverfew and evening primrose completed this colourscape. Across the path, around a terra-cotta sundial, were *Romneya coulteri, Geranium* 'Ann Folkard,' *Stipa gigantea,* nigella, flowering garlic, and verbascum. Her plant-ings are layered for seasonal variation as well as contrasting colours.

"With garden design, one has so many factors to consider and then you have to understand it will never be static—but that's the fun of it...talk about 'art in motion!' By September I'm craving paint on a canvas that stays still and doesn't need watering." Despite being pulled along two different artistic paths, Elizabeth Kerfoot manages to keep a balanced, creative life.

The Garden of Elsie and Ernie Lythgoe

Ernie and Elsie Lythgoe have lived at their lakefront property for over forty years. In the early spring a forsythia bush is full of blooms while narcissus and pulsatillas spread naturally down the slate path to the lake.

I never took gardening seriously until I married," admitted Ernie Lythgoe with a laugh. "And I married late." Now a determined ninety-three years young, Ernie still gardens every day in his one-acre garden on the border of Elk Lake Park, outside Victoria. Having been retired for twenty-seven years, Ernie said, "I couldn't have found a better hobby."

Ernie and Elsie Lythgoe moved to Elk Lake from Nanaimo and before that the Interior, where they both taught school. It was the early '50s and land outside the city was cheaper. They cleared part of the Douglas fir forest, built a house, and dug two wells for water, since, at that time, they were too far from Victoria to be connected to the city water supply. Despite aches and pains that come with decades of gardening, Ernie and Elsie continue to work their one acre. Their son, Erik,

mows the lawn, runs their compost chipper, and helps with the heavy work. They still maintain a substantial vegetable garden, rhododendron collection, and woodland garden, but their specialty is rock and alpine plants.

"Elsie was the rock gardener and expert. I did the hard work but as for plants, everything that flowered was a 'petunia' to me," said Ernie. Elsie's knowledge came from her early years growing up on a farm in the West Kootenays. "My mother died when I was eleven," she recalled. "So I had to run the farm, planting vegetables and harvesting too. We had to walk a mile to school and back, and that is when I first started to identify wild flowers."

Ernie remembers his youth as a mountain climber but he never noticed plants. Then he began to read books about the great plant explorers and became interested in rhododendrons. "In

*K*nown as an excellent alpine grower, Ernie Lythgoe still gardens in his nineties. *Shown here:* Primula marginata *in the rock wall.*

landscaping a place of this size you need large flowering shrubs, like rhododendrons, not just alpines," he explained. But it was alpines that led the Lythgoes to the Vancouver Island Rock & Alpine Garden Society (VIRAGS).

Through VIRAGS they met the great plantsman Ed Lohbrunner, who ran a nursery supplying conifers and alpines to garden experts worldwide. Throughout their long, enduring friendship, Ed, Elsie, and Ernie went on plant collecting expeditions in the mountains of the Rockies, the Kootenays, and closer to home on Vancouver Island. Ed was forever giving the Lythgoes seeds or cuttings of new plants. He called them his insurance, because if he lost the original plant he knew where he could find another.

Ernie Lythgoe was and is a superb grower. He has a greenhouse where he pots specialty alpines for showing, and cold frames for hardening out tender plants. The Lythgoes have won so many trophies that VIRAGS has given them an honourary life membership. They also have long-standing international connections to the British Alpine Garden Society, the Scottish Rock and Alpine Group, and the American Rock Garden Society. "We never miss our local VIRAGS meeting," said Elsie and Ernie together. "We still trade and collect plants with other members."

When the Lythgoes planted their garden, they built a south-facing, vertical rock wall for the alpines. The watering system in the lawn drains towards the lake. This is ideal for rock and alpine plants that require natural water from surface drainage. An annual sprinkling of bonemeal helps feed these special plants.

In the centre of the south-facing rock wall is a planting of *Helianthemum apenninum, Anemone drummondii, Tanacetum densum* subsp. *amani, Aquilegia alpina,* grey *Dianthus* 'Little Jock,' and tight clumps of campanula and *Genista villarsii* clinging to the rock face. In a semi-shaded section of the rockery, Japanese maples, dwarf blue spruce, cotoneaster, and *Corydalis lutea* vie for space. There is year-round colour in this alpine garden.

In the woodland garden, hybrid and species rhododendrons shade an assortment of spring bulbs and an extensive fern collection. A great drift of *Fritillaria meleagris* stands out amid native trilliums and erythroniums, both white and pink forms. Later in the season, ferns such as maidenhair, adder's tongue, ostrich, deer, sword, chain, and several species of polypodium provide a woodland ground cover. In this part of the garden the Lythgoes mulch heavily to cut down on summer watering and weeds.

Every year Ernie spreads ten yards of homemade compost. "There is only one spadeful of garden loam before you hit hard pan clay, so mulching is essential to maintain moisture, especially in the summer. We are lucky though, we have two wells that people think are ornamental but we need the extra water during the dry spells."

Beside a decorative well cover is *Rhododendron marinus* 'Koster,' with native wild ginger (*Asarum caudatum*), false bugbane (*Trautvetteria caroliniensis var. occidentalis*), false mitrewort (*Tiarella laciniata*), and starflower (*Smilacina stellata*). Along the lakefront is a thicket of alder, willow, birch, blackberry, thimbleberry, ocean spray, and snowberry. In the foreground the Lythgoes have planted an azalea walk with large clumps of Japanese iris, calla lilies, and monbretia.

"Of course we have problems with rabbits and deer, but we try and grow plants they don't like. Everywhere you look there is always something in bloom," he said pointing out the pulsatillas just starting to open below the bright yellow spring forsythia. In the summer, the silver-leafed, pineapple-scented, *Cytisus battandieri* with yellow flowers will be of interest. Nearby, a tiny pond was full with water hawthorn, water fern, and lilies. Even the tall Douglas fir trees were clothed in climbing roses and *Hydrangea petiolaris*.

"I don't know when I had time to work," said Ernie. "There is always too much to do in the garden."

Ernie built a south-facing rock wall for his special alpine plants. They are watered by run-off from the upper lawn.

The Garden of June Mayall

*J*une Mayall enjoyed working with the late Tommy Taylor to develop an outstanding collection of ferns, alpines and flowering rhododendrons and azaleas.

June Mayall has an informal garden on Ten Mile Point without pretext or pretension—much like the woman herself. "I don't do 'drifts' or coordinated colours," she explained. "I'm still learning." Her warmth and creative eye permeate her home and garden and despite her personal denigrations, the garden works beautifully.

June bought her home in the fall of 1979 with her partner, botanist emeritus Dr. Tommy Taylor, an expert on ferns. Dr. Taylor, originally from Ontario, is the author of many botanical texts, including the book *The Ferns and Fern Allies of B.C.* He brought his fern collection from his property at Lost Lake or "Teanook," many of which are rare. June pointed out one fern collected on the Broken Islands that appeared to be two different species of *Polypodium* on the same frond. Since the death of Dr. Taylor in 1983, June has done her utmost to protect and maintain this important fern collection.

"When we bought this house, there was a large ornamental plum in the front and a few old rhododendrons. Of interest was the enormous Monterey cypress in the back which is growing north of its normal range. We collected slate from Port Renfrew for the paths and put in exposed aggregate slabs. Tommy brought rhododendrons and azaleas from his garden and we planted them in the front in the semi-shade to soften the horizontal lines of the house. I put in the single pink *Camellia sasanqua*. On the sunny side, we built the rockery for all the alpine plants." *Rhodohypoxis, Gentiana, Lewisia,* and *Dryas* in tiny tufts thrive in the rockery.

June is an active member of the Rock and Alpine Club and her garden is often open to gardening clubs who come to experience the interesting collection of hardy plants. She is also an active member of the Victoria Natural History Society. Every week she walks in the wild with a group, and volunteers regularly at Beacon Hill Park in the Rock and Alpine Garden. Her garden reflects these interests. Native currant bushes and *Mahonia acanthifolia* attract hummingbirds, and her tall grass is a haven for young quail.

The actual property is two-thirds of an acre with the sloping back lot left wild. Native Garry oaks and wild flowers such as *Allium cernuum, Brodiaea*

June does not "do colour schemes," but enjoys mixing all colours as is shown in this simple spring planting of rock roses, narcissus, tulips and pansies.

coronaria, *Erythronium oregonum*, *Dodecatheon hendersonii*, *Camassia leichtlinii*, *Ranunculus occidentalis*, and *Collinsia grandiflora* grow among the tall grass. June is determined to keep out the introduced broom (*Cytisus scoparius*) and she grows native lilies from seed to reintroduce them into the wild.

Bordering the wild garden is a rockery with an enormous *Exochorda* x *macrantha* 'The Bride' dripping over the rock wall into which tiny sedums and sempervivums are tucked. Dwarf fruit trees were planted in the flat lawn and June is continually working on the depth of soil in her vegetable garden. "As much as I love my garden, I don't want it to run my life. Over the years I have been reducing the size of the vegetable garden and planting more flowers." June's children and grandchildren live throughout B.C. and she visits them regularly.

For ten years she had help from Neil Knowlton, a very thorough landscape consultant who now writes the monthly garden tips column in the Victoria Horticultural Society newsletter. Neil first worked for Dr. Taylor at Teanook and then continued to look after the garden following Dr. Taylor's death. "Neil helped tremendously in this garden," June remarked. "He sculpted the beds into a continuous curve and cleared the exposed rock outcrops for proper planting, which are now full of tall perennials bordered by primulas and *Limnanthes douglasii*. He is a master at compost and brought up the depth of soil everywhere."

Neil remembers June's garden fondly and remarked on its unique quality of having so many growing conditions in such a small space. "The garden has almost prairie conditions at the top of the hill with a wetland at the bottom. In between are sunny and shady conditions with exposed rock outcrops for visual interest. Both Tommy and June had a sense of the natural landscape while making the garden, and it shows today."

June now does most of the gardening herself, with occasional help. She is always adding and moving plants. "Every year is different. As a conservationist I try and make as little impact on the earth as possible. I don't spray with anything stronger than lime sulphur and I mulch the plants with compost and manure as much as possible. I feel I have a responsibility here. Man is going to interfere with the earth. So let us do it in a creative way."

The back section of Jane Mayall's garden is left wild with native bulbs and Garry oaks, a haven for birds and other wildlife.

The Garden of Renate and Herb Mayr

*R*enate and Herb Mayr are superb gardeners and plant collectors. Against a shady back wall they combine bamboo, hostas, ferns, Solomon's seal and ornamental grasses to great effect.

Renate and Herb Mayr are very disciplined gardeners. In an average city lot they grow a large collection of unusual plants. Herb is the plant propagator and builder while Renate is the designer and weeder. They both prune and are equally delighted by each flowering success.

"I am a perfectionist," said Renate, which explains why she doesn't open her garden to all the gardening groups anymore. "I would be down on my hands and knees for ten hours a day, three weeks prior to the tour. I don't like a messy garden, but my back could not take it. We had to cut back."

A bronze heron is the focal point in this collection of foliage. It would take many visits to see all there is to see in this garden. Renate is constantly adding to and rearranging the garden.

Herb and Renate moved to their present home in 1963 from Ontario. "We were strictly marigold gardeners then," they said. When their daughter started school, Renate had more time to read and she discovered the books of Beth Chatto. "That was it," she said. "I've been hooked on foliage ever since." In 1981 they joined the Geranium and Fuschia Club, propagating plants from seed, importing unusual varieties, and growing plants from cuttings in their greenhouse. They now grow fuschias and geraniums on a small commercial basis once a year for the University of Victoria plant sale.

It was not until 1987 that they planted their sunny garden in the vacant lot next to their house. The cold winter of 1989 killed two-thirds of it, including all their hebes, eucalyptus, and other tender plants. Because of Renate's continuing back problems they sold the lot, donating most of the remaining plants to their daughter, but keeping some mature shrubs for a new, smaller garden. The result is stunning.

Their back garden is a series of perennial borders under the shade of enormous Garry oaks with a background of yews and cedar hedging to the north. A hand-hewn, naturally-weathered, split-cedar fence protects the garden to the east. Against the fence flowered *Clematis viticella* 'Eto-ile Violette' grows next to the mauve Chinese *Wisteria sinensis*. In front, for foliage contrast, is *Sambucus racemosa* 'Sutherland,' Joe Pye weed, a large-leafed saxifrage, a tiny evergreen potentilla, succulents, white campanula, a white miniature rose ('Popcorn'), the 'Bowles' purple wallflower, *Geranium macrorrhizum* with deep magenta flowers, and white *Osteospermum* 'Whirligig.' For grey foliage contrast are stocks, dusty miller, dianthus, and lychnis (both white and pale pink forms). Of special interest are *Paeonia tenuifolia* with finely-cut leaves, a soft blue *Eryngium* 'Donards' and a tiny prostrate *Epilobium glabellum*.

Beside the border is a tiny log play house that Herb built for his daughter when she was five. The house is now used as a storage shed with a shady planting of *Polygonum cuspidatum*, hostas, ferns, and deep purple *Heuchera* 'Palace Purple'

beside it. *Robinia pseudoacacia* 'Frisia' towers above in golden contrast to the green cedar hedging. The Mayrs are very conscious of yellow in the garden. Renate uses yellow foliage plants throughout, such as *Hosta* 'August Moon,' *Carex elata* 'Bowles Golden,' and *Euphorbia seguieriana*, but avoids yellow and grey together. The odd exception is a rare, yellow-flowering and grey-leafed stachys: Renate is a consummate collector of the unusual.

In one corner I noticed *Dictamus albus*, both white and pink forms. In another planting, beside the blue-tinged *Mahonia* 'Winter Sun' and *Hosta* 'Halcyon' was an evergreen *Begonia* 'Sutherlandii' with pale coral-coloured flowers in contrast to the red-leafed Japanese maple beside it. Across the path was a newly acquired tiny variegated *Helxine soleirollii variegata* (baby's tears) beside the rare fern *Athyrium filix-femina* 'Frizelliae.'

Throughout the garden are conifers and deciduous trees planted for vertical interest with vines climbing up them. In the front, a silver-leafed pear is intertwined with the deep purple *Clematis viticella* 'Etoile Violette.' In the back, the Garry oaks are covered in the large-leafed Dutchman's Pipe climber, while hop vines cover the cedar hedge. A pergola of roses, ivy, and clematis separates the main garden from the vegetable plot, potting area, and greenhouse, where *Crambe cordifolia* blooms prolifically by an ivy-covered pillar. "I want to create a sense of abundance," exclaimed Renate.

The Mayrs prune heavily in order to fit so many plants in such a small space. They mulch spring and fall with a mixture of leaf mold, manure, bone meal, and canola meal to feed the existing clay soil. They do not spray diseased plants because of their cats, preferring to cut back fungus-riddled foliage. All the plants are well watered with a watering system that Herb is continually adjusting for height as plants grow.

The front garden has a pond and place for boggy plants. Water lilies, water iris, water hawthorn, and water fern (which is invasive and must be watched) grow in the pond. Bordering it under a weeping birch, Japanese maple and pendulous corkscrew beech is an interesting perennial mix that includes candelabra primulas, variegated as-

$\mathscr{R}$enate uses yellow foliage to bring light to shady spots. The yellow Euonymus fortunii *'Emerald and Gold' is mirrored across the path in the new foliage of the Japanese maple. The pink of the tulip mirrors the pink of the blooms of the magnolia.*

trantias, hostas, potentilla 'Miss Wilmot,' *Mimulus lewisii*, rue 'Afgani', spiraea 'Bridal Veil,' Himalayan poppies, yellow feverfew, *Trollius* 'Alabaster' and a new *Linaria triornithophora* from the University of British Columbia.

On the other side of the house, replacing a long strip of lawn, are two newly-created meandering borders full of bulbs and perennials in variegated,

yellow, and other unusual forms which the Mayrs have acquired through the Hardy Plant Group of the Victoria Horticultural Society, and by sharing with gardening friends. Renate is a volunteer at the Friends of the University of Victoria Gardens and she travels regularly to hunt down rare specimens on her wish list. "After all," laughed Renate, "the chase is half the fun."

The Garden of George and Ann Nation

*G*eorge and Ann Nation are very active gardeners in the community. Maidenhair ferns, Japanese maples and geraniums border a lily pond with Dierama pulcherrimum *in the foreground. In the background, a dramatic perennial border of poppies, peonies and lilies sweeps to the sea.*

When George and Ann Nation moved to Victoria from Montreal, George brought a box of plants with him on the plane. "We had a rock garden in Montreal," he said. "I brought a few choice plants with me." Now a life member of the Vancouver Island Rock and Alpine Growers Society (VIRAGS), for which he still judges, George Nation tends his rock plants and his rose collection. His wife, Ann, started the Victoria garden tours for the Victoria Conservatory of Music and ran this successful fundraiser for ten years. Although retired from a leadership

A magnificent hydrangea provides plenty of fall colour.

71

role, Ann is still involved in the annual event. This year, fifteen hundred people visited the Nation garden, one of thirteen on the tour. While George ran the plant sale on the front deck, Ann assisted with a formal tea in their back garden.

Their garden overlooks the Olympic Peninsula, with a delightful statue of a sea lion guarding the seaside entrance. "We were very lucky when we came here sixteen years ago," they said. "The people that built the house in the '40s preferred garden beds with informal curves, and so do we. The beds were where they are now, but we have made them larger and changed the plant material." In the back garden, the Nations removed a bed of coniferous shrubs shading the house. They kept the three existing ponds but extended rockeries around the pools. A cement path leading to the sea was changed to brick and they put in concrete slab steps to the pebble beach with a terraced planting on either side. Over time a greenhouse and back patio were built.

The entrance required more work. They closed off part of the circular driveway, planting holly, magnolias, rhododendrons, tree peonies, and late-flowering *Cornus kousa* for privacy from the street. To break up the monotony of the exposed aggregate, tufts of creeping thyme, dianthus, and hardy geraniums were planted in the cracks. George has trough gardens with gentians, lewisias, helichrysum, and sedums for viewing on patio chairs. A front deck was built with a pergola for wisteria and *Clematis armandii*. In the early summer, the scented rose 'Maigold' blooms by the front door against the warmth of the brick facia.

From the front garden to the oceanside one follows a shaded gravel path through a planting of trilliums, primulas, and ferns. The path opens up to a spectacular planting of white calla lilies which George divided to keep them flowering. Across the path, towards the sea, is a lily-studded pond with a centre island featuring a sculpture of the Nations' grandson by a local artist, Peggy Walton Packard. Surrounding half of the pond in full sun is a recently replanted rockery with rhodohypoxis (white and deep pink forms), phlox ('Rose Cushion'), rock roses, saxifrage, pink flowering *Oxalis ad-*enophylla, *Chrysanthemum halendosum,* and lady's-mantle.

Under the shade of an ornamental plum garden, designer Claudia Peterson put in a slate path behind the pond with hostas, hardy geraniums, yellow daylilies, astilbes, and perennial forget-me-nots leading to the white flowering *Hoheria lyallii*, a tender deciduous tree with blue-green leaves.

Claudia Peterson is called upon by the Nations for special projects. This year when they removed their carport to build a proper garage, Claudia completed the entire east side's landscaping in five days. Claudia's mother did the finishing brickwork; her brother built the frame for the rose pergola; and Claudia, with one other helper, brought in the paving stone, gravel, and soil to build a sloping bed of rhododendrons, trilliums (*Trillium nivale, T. ovatum, T. rivale, T. tomentosum, T. grandiflorum*), wild ginger, and a Judas tree. Besides special projects, the Nations have help one-and-a-quarter days a week with lawn mowing and weeding. Still, in this half-acre garden there is a great deal of maintenance.

"Our neighbour, an agronomist, explained that because of our seaside location, the lawn would be very shallow rooted. Salt counteracts lime. Last year, at his suggestion, we added thirty bags of lime to the lawn and it has made a tremendous difference. Besides that we compost everything using a shredder." Ann adds fertilizer (20-20-20) to the perennials, but compost and water are the most important additions to clay soil. "If the garden dries out," explained George, "the soil is so hard you cannot even put a pitchfork in it." The Nations have a watering system throughout the beds, including the rose garden.

George began his rose collection with an order of forty-five roses from Aberdeen, Scotland. Today the hybrid tea roses make an elegant presentation around a raised sundial, beside an old plum tree. There is the deep red 'National Trust,' the golden yellow 'Korresia,' the pale pink 'Fairy Dancer,' and the creamy white 'Pascali,' to name just a few. Ann was given a collection of old roses from the Board of the Conservatory of Music. Growing on the new pergola are scented

Japanese maples and tuberous begonias surround the lily-studded pond. In the centre island are ornamental grasses and ferns.

roses such as the hybrid perpetual 'Baron Girod de l'Ain,' hybrid musk 'Buff Beauty,' floriferous pale pink 'Felicia' and 'Boule de Neige' with crimson buds and scented cream-coloured flowers.

From the rose garden your eye follows the lawn past an enormous weeping willow to a perennial border that sweeps to the sea. The Nations grow vegetables and herbs quite successfully on the oceanside. Lettuce, tomatoes, artichokes, fennel, and basil thrive, but every year they add more flowers. Hardy geraniums, evening primroses, heathers, *Iris pseudacorus*, *Dierama pendulum*, asters, alliums, and lychnis are all salt-tolerant perennials, while shrubs such as escalonia, hardy fuschia, and *Rosa rugosa* grow right in the spray zone.

The Nations do not fuss about colour placement. "We change the borders every year," said Ann, "but height is my big worry. I keep moving the shorter plants to the front but then they receive more sun and grow taller—it is frustrating. My mother had perfect perennial borders because every year they took out every plant, divided each clump and replanted." Ann sighed, "I keep hoping the borders will stay put but the look changes annually."

With that, George and Ann went back to their weeding, in preparation for a group of gardeners visiting the following week from California.

The Garden of Phoebe Noble

A rustic bench in front of a cedar hedge is bordered by honesty and sweet cicely in the internationally acclaimed garden of Phoebe Noble. Now in her eightieth year, Phoebe is very involved in the Victoria gardening community.

*P*hoebe Noble specializes in hardy geraniums. She has over seventy species growing in her Deep Cove garden, one of which is named after her. *Geranium* x *oxonianum* 'Phoebe Noble' is available in nurseries internationally. Every year Phoebe visits the gardens of England to observe new plantings and visit old friends. When I visited Phoebe in the spring she was wearing a pink Chanel suit, having just returned from a meeting in town, and was unloading kelp fertilizer into a wheelbarrow. We stopped to chat on a wooden bench overlooking the vegetable garden and perennial borders.

"My grandfather built a house here in 1906. My husband and I moved to the property in the 1960s and, in the '70s, we planted the orchard." After her husband died, Phoebe retired from teaching mathematics at the University of Victoria and turned her attention to the garden. Her daughter, Sandra, continues in her father's tradition and manages the large, heavily-mulched vegetable garden in her time off from work in Victoria.

Phoebe Noble, a woman of generous smiles and ceaseless energy, looks after the remaining garden on the two-acre property. She still mows the lawns, but now has help from a handyman with some of the heavier jobs. The essence of Phoebe's gardening is mulching. "I mulch using compost, manure, wood chips, shredded plants, whatever I can get. I usually get two or three loads of manure every season." Water is a limiting factor, and mulching holds moisture and prevents desiccation, especially in the hot summer months.

Phoebe's garden is a series of meandering perennial borders surrounded by well-planned thickets and cedar hedging. "I planted everything

*P*hoebe Noble lets leeks go to seed amid 'Queen Elizabeth' roses, iberis and hardy geraniums. Phoebe uses conifers at the end of the border for vertical accent.

but the original Douglas firs and the old crabapple tree. The first thing I did was plant more firs for privacy and wind break. I feel a garden has to be private. The northeast winds in February are bitterly cold and drying. I'm replacing this planting of cypresses. They were a mistake and require too much pruning—Portuguese laurels would be better."

There are permanent sprinklers in the lower waterfront garden but the main upper garden is always changing and so is watered manually. "Everything I do and plan is to reduce the amount of work and make the garden more maintenance-free. That is why I like hardy geraniums. They are great ground covers." In the orchard, under the fruit trees are mass plantings of *Geranium macrorrhizum*, all grown from one original plant.

"I like to concentrate on foliage, texture, and shape," Phoebe explained. "Contrasts are important, too." Behind us is a planting with the spiky foliage of the globe artichoke, combined with the round leaf of *Geranium pratense* and an early spring flowering of the elegant 'Queen of Night' black tulips. Phoebe also layers plants. *Geranium tuberosum* is combined with rhubarb; when one plant is finished the other takes over.

"I do watch my colours," Phoebe admitted. "*Geranium psilostemon* is a strong magenta colour. I combine it with a pink astrantia and am now looking for a dark purple-blue, maybe delphiniums, but slugs are a problem. In the yellow border I use grey as a contrast and hotter colours in the fall. Orange tiger lilies bloom under the *Robinia pseudoacacia* 'Frisia.' Behind the *Euphorbia griffithii* is a clump of golden hosta and I plant lots of golden Spanish broom. For contrast, I have a planting of the black, grasslike *Ophiopogon planiscapus* 'Nigrescens' combined with white *Anemone blanda* in spring, white *Campanula lactiflora* 'Pouffe' in the summer, and the white form of the fall crocus in autumn. There is also a purple, crimson, red, and grey border similar to one I saw at Hidcote in England.

"I am always moving things and enlarging the borders because I need more room. I keep experimenting with hardy geraniums, moving shade-loving varieties to the sun and drought-tolerant species to wet spots. I like to stretch their limits. Year-round colour is important to me but I prefer to leave the colour in the garden rather than pick it for indoors. All winter *Viburnum bodnantense* 'Dawn' blooms outside my bedroom window, and in the spring, the clematis start to show. Every shrub that is a decent size has a vine climbing on it. I just bought a white flowering form of *Aconitum helmslianum*. I enjoy collecting unusual plants."

Phoebe is very involved in the gardening community and will be hosting Penelope Hobhouse this summer, whom she met years ago in England. Phoebe is an Honourary Director of the Gardens of Government House, one of the original three chosen by Lieutenant Governor David Lam to redesign the gardens at Government House. "I promised his Honour I would stay until the garden was organized and now, with over a hundred active volunteers, and many dedicated subcommittees, I can say that it is very organized." Phoebe recently lectured to the volunteers on the use of mulches and now meets with other executive members only once or twice a month. She hopes to devote more time to her own garden in the new year.

As we walked back to my car, Phoebe generously offered me two pots of *Geranium macrorrhizum* for my own garden. I couldn't help but notice that I was parked on a roadside planting of *Allium moly*, *Limnanthes douglasii*, and *Oenothera lamarckiana*. When I apologized, Phoebe reassured me with a laugh: "My neighbours tease me," she said. "They ask when am I going to start planting in the asphalt."

Phoebe Noble is a great believer in mulching to cut down on weeding. Clematis viticella climbs on an old rose (an original planted c. 1910) which in turn leans on a privet hedge beside a deep-blue clump of Japanese iris. There is no room for weeds in this layered planting.

The Garden of Joan Outerbridge

oan Outerbridge is creating a bird and butterfly sanctuary in the city. Three out of nine acres are under intense cultivation. Shown here, the main lily pond bordered by irises with an island of bulrushes, a haven for waterfowl.

I'm not the manicured type," said Joan Out-erbridge, pointing to her work boots, work pants, plaid shirt and padded vest. "And neither is this garden. 'Shangri-la,' that's what I call it, is a naturalistic garden—a place where you can relax while enjoying the plants and bird life." As she spoke, the redwing blackbirds called back and forth—an unusual sound for the city. Violet-green swallows darted in and out of their raised nesting boxes in a courting frenzy. "Ah," sighed Joan, "if I could be reincarnated I'd love to be a violet-green swallow."

*B*uddleias and daisies are planted in large masses to attract butterflies to "Shangri-la" in the late summer.

Joan Outerbridge (who prefers to be called Jo-ann), was born in Bermuda and lived there most of her life, although, she said, "If I had known about Victoria I would have moved here earlier." As a child, Joan collected insects. She later majored in landscape design at Ambler College, now part of Temple University in Pennsylvania. She met her husband in Bermuda and married at the age of fifty. Widowed in 1976, Joan immigrated to Canada in 1987 and began her garden that summer. Now owner of a nine-acre parcel of land in residential Saanich, Joan has created a bird and butterfly sanctuary with feeding stations, nesting boxes, and special plants to encourage wildlife.

Joan's first job was to excavate a large, natural clay pond with a centre island for waterfowl. In the bulrushes of the small island, which Joan reaches by rowboat, are a pair of mallards tending to a brood, one of seven resident nesting pairs. Joan's house overlooks this pond so that she can watch this year's babies, which she calls "my grandchildren."

Joan mows her own lawn and has planted most of the garden herself, raising plants from seed or by cuttings or going to demolition sales. She does not drive but is a regular bus traveller to nurseries. "I have help now on a regular basis and hire machine operators to move the big rocks," she explained. Watering is done with hoses from water spigots throughout the property. Only three of the nine acres are under intense cultivation; still, it is an enormous undertaking and Joan is expanding the garden all the time.

Our tour began along the pond where Joan, a member of the Heather Club, has an excellent collection of heathers, including 'Myretoun Ruby,' 'Eileen Porter,' 'Kramer's Red,' 'Robert Chapman,' and 'Boskoop,' the latter two having coloured foliage. They all provide winter colour.

In the spring, primroses, scilla, phlox, and aubrietias are favourites at Shangri-la. Beside a cascading rock waterfall is a seventy-two-year-old 'Golden Nectar' plum that Joan salvaged. Below the plum is a curved bench for contemplation, and a Japanese-style bridge overlooking the pond. Gold-leafed Creeping Jenny, *Ajuga* 'Burgundy

Lace,' sempervivums, and ornamental grasses are used in the hot scree sites for colour and texture. Joan has a five-horse-power pump that circulates the water from the main pond to the two other ponds and waterfalls. It is a simple system that works beautifully, and one is able to view the waterfalls from several angles.

Beyond "Placid Pool" near the old plum is Joan's new rock and alpine garden. Gentians in cerulean blue, apricot pink lewisias, and creamy yellow *Cheiranthus* are a few of the alpines Joan has recently added. "I try and blend colours," Joan said, "but I don't have much red because it is hard to blend. I'm constantly reading and learning," she laughed. Her scree mixture of one part sand/gravel, one part loam, one part peat moss is the perfect growing medium for alpines. Beyond the alpine garden is a luscious bamboo hedge and large planting of pampas grass (*Cortaderia*) which the quail like for protection from hawks. Goldfinches love thistles and so Joan lets them seed in the thickets of blackberries.

"Deer have become a major problem, but it is no wonder with all the development surrounding my property. I finally had to fence a portion of the garden from the deer." On a sloped field Joan is clearing rocks to plant a wildflower area. She has saved camas seeds, shooting stars, chocolate lilies and fawn lilies, both *Erythronium oregonum*, and *E. revolutum*. She proudly shows me her new rototiller, which she is using to till the field for the first time. As we walk, Rufous hummingbirds that migrate from Mexico and California dive and buzz around us. They love the native red currant, *Ribes sanguineum*, which is planted throughout the garden. Joan has also seen the more unusual Anna's hummingbird which winters on Vancouver Island.

Beyond the wildflower garden is a snowberry thicket to the "Secret Pond" where Siberian iris, water iris, and Japanese iris (*I. ensata*) bloom in the summer. The butterfly garden is beside the "Secret Pond" with many species of *Buddleia* or butterfly bush. Joan grew the purple, pink, and white forms of *B. davidii* from cuttings and has lovely specimens of *B. globosa*, the more unusual yellow-orange form with a ball-like flower. She also

Rhododendron 'Elizabeth' (Wisley strain) by a Chinese bridge. Mrs. Outerbridge does not use much red in her garden as she finds it difficult to blend with other colours.

grows *B. alternifolia*, the fountain butterfly bush with lavender flowers. These butterfly bushes attract a variety of butterflies, as well as hummingbirds. Eventually, she hopes the Monarch butterfly will survive at Shangri-la. Joan urges other gardeners to plant *Asclepias* (milkweed), a non-invasive border plant which is the only plant where the female insects lay their eggs.

Once more we return to the main pond and take the shady rhododendron walk back to the house. By a Chinese bridge is the *R.* 'Hawk Crest,' a lovely lemon-yellow colour, and *R.* 'Elizabeth,' a deep red. Horsetail and morning glory are a constant problem. Joan admits, "I've learned some hard lessons but I look at the garden as my 'Unfinished Symphony.' I'm working on getting it put into a private trust. I want people to come here. Last year, we had twelve hundred visitors in one weekend, but I also want the birds and butterflies to have a place to go."

I left Joan in her new greenhouse repotting a superb collection of lewisias in full bloom. If I could be reincarnated I, too, would like to be a violet-green swallow in Joan Outerbridge's Shangri-la.

The Garden of Peggy Walton Packard and Amy Walton

*P*eggy Packard incorporates her unique sculptures in intimate corners throughout the garden. In the background, crimson Virginia creeper, climbing beans, bamboo, solidago, Marguerite daisies and nasturtiums provide autumn colour.

When the Dead Poets' Society of Victoria hosts its midsummer's night frolic they meet in the garden of Peggy Walton Packard and Amy Walton. When the Saanich International Folk Dancers Club have their annual celebration they, too, use the house and garden of Peggy Walton Packard and Amy Walton. When Peggy Walton Packard's sculpture students have their yearly show it is also in the home and garden that has been in the Walton family for almost a century.

"The Barn," as Peggy and Amy's house is called, is all that remains of the original four-acre farm bought by their father in 1912. The barn-carriage house was used as a double garage, and the stable, now Peg's sculpture studio, sheltered a Jersey cow. The original family home with privet hedges, lawn tennis court, and a thousand chickens is gone but "The Barn" property encompasses some of the orchard and kitchen garden where Peggy and Amy grew up. When their mother died in 1963 the original house was sold and Peggy and Amy (and Peggy's two young children) moved into "The Barn."

Since then, they have created a garden that feels like home. They are not plant collectors or devout horticulturists but are women who have created an appealing, creative landscape by the sweat of their brow. As Peggy said, "The garden rolls with the seasons." From the early spring bluebells and grape hyacinths that run amok, to the fall scarlet Virginia creeper and nasturtiums that entwine themselves among the vegetables, it is a garden of intimate spaces and surprising features.

In the centre of the garden is an enormous, ancient Garry oak from which hangs a swing suspended from a tree branch thirty feet above it. When I asked Peggy how she got it up there, she laughed and said she borrowed a ladder, admitting that "it was pretty dicey all the same." Amy just rolled her eyes. It is Amy who mows the lawn, trims the edges, and plants the vegetables, but it is Peggy who is the overall designer, digger and pruner.

"I built all the fish ponds, hauling all those rocks in my Mini Minor." When I point out that some of the rocks are indeed enormous, Peggy looked serious, "It is no wonder my back hurts," she says, wincing as she shifts in her seat to ease the ache. "Amy and I built the winding slate path from the back garden gate to the studio. We

Bluebells seed freely among the tulips and narcissus in the spring garden of Amy Walton and Peggy Walton Packard.

hauled the slate from nearby Port Renfrew and split it wafer thin to make it stretch." An outdoor fireplace was constructed from the original barn foundation rocks and all the brickwork they did themselves, scrounging bricks "shamelessly" wherever they could be found.

Central to Peggy's garden design is the placement of her sculptures. Trained at the Academy of Fine Arts in Pennsylvania, Peggy has taught sculpture once a week for decades to a faithful group of enthusiastic artists. She still does commissioned pieces. The models for the sculptures are often her own grandchildren or neighbours. "I love children," exclaimed Peggy; and it shows, for surely this garden could be a model for the children's classic story *The Secret Garden*. A young boy holds his hand out to feel the drip from a bamboo pole, another child sits in the crook of a century-old apple tree gazing to the sky, while a young woman strolls through the spring tulips, her dress rippling in the breeze. These evocative figures bring human scale to the garden and provide a focal point to the jungle of foliage.

"I am always looking for possibilities," said Peggy. "We always used what we had and hoped it would work out." This is a philosophy that runs through everything Peggy has done, from being a single mother and surviving cancer at a young age, to designing her garden. "It looks rustic," said Peggy, "but I like it that way. I should cut down the filberts that shade the vegetable garden and the volunteer birch tree that is now thirty-feet-high, but I changed my mind because they seem happy there."

The garden is a mixture of perennials bordered by hedges of bamboo and cedars. The long lot is broken up by Peggy's tableaux. Each pond creates its own picture with Japanese maples and rhododendrons. There are sitting benches for viewing and old painted wooden lawn chairs for resting and chatting. It is a garden for wandering and contemplation in the English cottage style, with mass plantings of larkspurs, peonies, and daylilies. Yellow Icelandic poppies, pale blue bachelor buttons, purple honesty, pink and white Japanese anemones, and white and mauve sweet rocket are allowed to seed freely among the herbs. In the summer even the Michaelmas daisies, Japanese lanterns, and nasturtiums are given free reign to sprout and climb among the dahlias and black-eyed Susans.

When I left the garden I noticed an old wicker basket minus its bottom, tacked ten feet up in a tree. "Oh that," said Peggy, "is for basketball. The grandchildren and I like to shoot a bit."

The Garden of Doris Page

*H*elleborus orientalis *grows here amid a backdrop of many species of snowdrop. Ms. Page's shady woodland garden is outstanding in the winter and early spring while most other gardens rest.*

When Doris Page bought her house and garden forty-five years ago, it lay in an open field beside a steeply wooded hill to the west, shaded by native firs and cedars, and on the east, by a small park of second-growth fir, maple, cedar, and dogwood. Salal, snowberry, ocean spray, red huckleberry, Oregon grape, and thimbleberry flourished here along with a groundcover of sword fern, vanilla leaf, starflower, twinflower, and *Goodyera menziesi* completing the woodland effect. The garden, now shaded by self-seeded maples, is packed with native and introduced plants that Doris seeded herself for a low-maintenance garden with emphasis on winter interest and fragrance.

When Penelope Hobhouse, noted British gar-

Doris Page worked tirelessly to protect the forest of Douglas firs and maple trees opposite her home. Her efforts were acknowledged when the municipality named the park in her honour.

den writer, visited Doris' garden several years ago she commented on the use of indigenous plant material. "I have seen many beautiful gardens in Victoria," said Mrs. Hobhouse, "but they could be found anywhere in England. Your garden has an interesting mix of native and non-native material. Why don't you promote native plants?"

"I have," Doris replied, "for the last forty years!"

Doris Page is known to most Victorians for her local television program on gardening. The show, "Island Country Garden," ran for eighteen years on CHEK TV. "When I had to go and have my other hip repaired I thought it was time to stop." Despite being troubled by arthritis, Doris still gardens using a walker. The day I arrived in late spring, she was busy pruning beneath an archway covered with ivy and the fragrant *Aktinidia kolomitka*. Walking up the driveway I could see an understorey planting of epimedium, sweet woodruff, native sword ferns and ostrich ferns, Oregon grape, bleeding hearts, with blooming Welsh poppies (both single and double) and bluebells (*Scilla nutans*) scattered about. The bluebells and poppies had seeded themselves up the woodland path that Doris built herself on the steep hillside.

I followed the driveway past the arching shrub rose *Rosa* 'Frühlingsgold' blooming with its fragrant single, pale yellow blossom. Doris showed me the damage done recently by deer eating the new growth on her Japanese anemones; luckily they had spared a spectacular pale pink single peony, *Paeonia mlokosewitschii* 'Mother of Pearl.' "No, they haven't eaten that," laughed Doris, "although their diet seems to become more varied every year."

Once settled inside her cosy cottage, Doris explained that the road running along her property was once a railway line. It is thought that her house may have originated from some parts of the station buildings, with extra rooms added by a former owner. "I've been told that people used to come on excursions from town to Cordova Bay to see the dogwoods in bloom. I've lost three dogwoods over the last five years due to the recently introduced fungus but there are still a few trees remaining." Doris' house was declared a

Scented Rosa 'Frühlingsgold' blooms in the early summer. Ms. Page found it to be one of the few roses that is shade tolerant.

heritage site by the municipality, and the native parkland across the street, which she fought long and hard to keep, is named Doris Page Park.

I asked Doris if she was always interested in gardens. "I remember my grandfather taking me into our tiny garden in Barrow, in the northwest corner of England. My father was killed in the First World War when I was just born, but my mother introduced me to wildflowers." As a young woman, Doris studied horticulture at Studley College in Warwickshire and ran a market garden. During the Second World War Doris returned to the college, supervising the outdoor practical work of the students; later, she ran the garden of

a wartime maternity hospital. After the war she helped two friends who were starting a small holding in the Isle of Mull, while she waited for a passage to Canada. Her mother had recently died and it was through friends of her mother's that she came to Victoria. Within weeks of her arrival she began to work for plantsman Ed Lohbrunner, for whom she continued to work for the next thirty-two years until her retirement in 1980.

"The pay was terrible," said Doris laughing, "but I owned my own house and the work was interesting. Ed Lohbrunner made his living as a landscaper but his international reputation was based on his extensive knowledge of native plants and skill with rock and alpines. He sent plants from his Lakeview Gardens Nursery to botanical gardens throughout the world, including Kew Gardens in England." It was Ed's brother, Joe, who built Doris' irrigation system and greenhouse which is, to this day, full of seedlings and cuttings for friends and society plant sales. During her years working for the Lohbrunners Doris developed her own reputation as a propagator and horticulturist.

Doris belongs to the Royal Horticultural Society, the Alpine Garden Society, and the Hardy Plant Society of England as well as the B.C. Hardy Plant Society, the Heather Society, and the Alpine Garden Society of B.C. These groups send out free seeds for propagation annually and Doris' garden is full of these plants. Over the years she has specialized in certain genera such as hardy geraniums, polygonums, species (i.e., wild) roses, euphorbias, and hellebores. "My garden was too shady for Ed's alpines but I brought home sick plants—'hospital trees' I called them. The crabapple is one. It's growing out of the grave of my old dog Rory and flowered beautifully this year," remembers Doris fondly. "Every plant was swapped back and forth and talked about—each one has memories."

As the shrubs and trees grew in the garden it slowly changed the microclimates within it, so some plants have dwindled and others disap-peared. Some memorable chance associations in the garden include the sight of pure white foxgloves in front of the native goatsbeard, a combination of yellow foxgloves (*Digitalis ambigua*), golden *Geranium psilostemon*, and the yellow frothy blooms of lady's-mantle; and in the fall you can admire a large *Parrotia persica* near an *Acer davidii* grown from seed. Doris remembers how the north side of the garden was lit up in a glorious glow.

As past president of the Victoria Horticultural Society for two terms (four years) her expertise is often called upon. She has written articles for British horticultural journals and still writes for the popular local gardening magazine, *The Island Grower*. Doris also supervises and helps maintain the Doris Page Winter Garden at the Horticultural Centre of the Pacific. There, students get hands-on experience working with plants and learning what Doris Page has always known: that a garden is more than just "colour."

"My aim for my own home was to have a low-maintenance garden so that I could stay here forever." A two-wheeled and one-handled wheelbarrow, a kneeling stool, electric mower, and electric chipper are aids that Doris hopes will enable her to keep active in the garden. As she says, "It is always easier to relax in someone else's garden... in one's own, one sees all the jobs waiting to be done." When I left, Doris returned to her pruning.

The Garden of Peter and Marylee Platt

Even in the snow, it is possible to see Peter and Marylee Platt's feeling for space, foliage and texture in their garden.

ardening has always been an integral part of Peter and Marylee Platt's life and marriage. When they moved from the east coast to Victoria in the mid-'60s, Marylee brought samples of the gas plant (*Dictamnus albus*) and bugbane (*Cimicifuga simplex* var. *racemosa*) from her mother's garden in Montreal. Twenty years later when their two children had grown and moved away, the Platts decided to leave their double Oak Bay lot to move to a smaller house and garden. They brought much of the garden with them. Rhododendrons twelve

In late summer an urn is surrounded by Alstromeria 'Light Hybrids' and brilliantly coloured Asian lilies. The urn was brought by the Platts from their former home in Montreal.

feet high were dug up and replanted. Peter's prize tufa rocks and alpine plants were carefully moved to their new location. "We couldn't take everything," explained Marylee, "but a few choice plants were too special to leave behind."

Their garden for the last twelve years was thought to have been the lawn tennis court for the original neighbouring estate. It is a flat site of large Garry oaks, enormous western red cedars, and maples which cast long shadows and absorb a great deal of moisture. "We were attracted to the lot," said Marylee, "because of the privacy it offered and the potential for a garden. There was little here when we came. The back garden had an enormous ornamental plum, and a large red rhododendron (R. 'Elizabeth') which we kept. But we pulled out all the tired old shrubs, montbretia, and Shasta daisies. A German friend helped us move our large *Rhododendron fictolacteum* that we got from Stuart Holland, R. 'Autumn Glow,' a blue ceanothus, and a *Prunus subhirtella* that is doing splendidly in the front."

The Platts are serious gardeners who know the value of good soil. They spent the first year designing beds and double trenching, adding sand, manure, and compost. "We wanted a low-maintenance garden," explained Marylee, "so shrubs and bulbs were the emphasis. Curves are important in an informal garden. You don't want to be able to see everything at one glance. Anticipation of what is beyond keeps the eye focused and interested."

In their second year the Platts tackled the east border removing a one hundred-foot stretch of English ivy. "Dr. Neville Grant was breaking up his garden and, with our trailer, we brought a *Eucryphia*, and mature azaleas and rhododendrons, all moved in the heat of August. We watered well and everything has flourished." Marylee has planted the sunnier portions of the border with grey hieraceums, lavender, and heathers, which follow early flowering drifts of snowdrops and daffodils. Himalayan poppies bloom in the late spring, with lilies in the summer and dahlias in the fall. There is always something happening in the low-maintenance borders.

In the front entrance, Marylee has her herbs and roses on one side of the path, with spires of rosemary echoing the cedar hedging behind. Peter, a long-time member of the Rock and Alpine Club, has his special tufa alpine garden on the other side, with tiny mounds of *Dryas*, *Pachystima*, and *Silene* amid alpine ferns, dwarf bulbs, and natives such as *Lewisia rediviva* collected on expeditions to mountains in the Interior and in Washington State. Peter went on trips with local plantsmen Ed Lohbrunner and Albert de Mezey to collect plants and rocks. He is always testing seeds and taking cuttings for friends and colleagues.

Both Peter and Marylee have backgrounds rich in gardening knowledge. Marylee studied horticulture in Groton, Massachusetts, at Lowthorpe College. When the Second World War broke out Marylee had to work to continue her studies. She learned by doing in the herb gardens of the college. "We took classes at M.I.T. in Gardening and Art and The Historical Treatment of Gardens. It was fascinating." Upon graduation Marylee returned to Canada and joined the WRENS, where she built the only Victory Garden in the navy. "We were the only naval base with fresh vegetables. We actually fed four hundred people fresh corn from our plot," laughed Marylee. When the war ended there were no landscape courses in Canada, so Marylee returned to the U.S. to study at Ambler College, and later worked in a firm in Philadelphia. "I wish now that I had studied landscape architecture," explained Marylee, "but it was not an option then."

Peter's family were great gardeners in Devon, England. They built a house in an old limestone quarry, which no doubt fuelled Peter's lifelong interest in rock gardens. Peter came to Canada to study chemical engineering at McGill University and was stationed in Ottawa after the war. He met Marylee at a cocktail party, where a mutual friend introduced them. "You two are made for each other," she said. "You both like music and gardening." Both Peter and Marylee laughed as they remembered.

When I ask them about their colour preferences in the garden they both say they dislike purple (but it was Peter who introduced the wall-

The white blooms of Rhododendron 'Lord Aberconway' with azalea R. schlippenbachii compliment a charming bird bath surrounded by the leaves of Cimicifuga and Ceanothus. Mrs. Platt planted white impatiens in the gap left by spring bulbs.

flower 'Bowles Purple' to Victoria via Doris Page and a local nursery). They like colours to blend and harmonize and they both emphasize foliage in the garden. Marylee designed a Japanese section in the shady back garden. Around a Tori gate built on an angle she has planted a short, a variegated and a tall ebony bamboo, with an understorey of hostas and native ferns. "Any garden can be made," said Marylee, "with time and effort."

The Platts are once again planning a move. Peter, now over eighty, finds the lawn a chore and so they are moving to a condominium close by. But they will be taking some of the tufa and alpines and a few other choice shrubs. "They are like old friends," explained Marylee. "We couldn't leave them."

The Garden of George Radford and Bruce Gibson-Bean

*G*eorge Radford and Bruce Gibson-Bean had a meticulously planned garden at "Bankview." While colour was important to the two, foliage was essential. Shown here, Solomon's seal, bleeding hearts, sweet rocket, hardy geraniums, Japanese anemones and many species of hostas.

George Radford and Bruce Gibson-Bean have an international reputation in the gardening world. Their garden has been featured in books by such gardening gurus as Rosemary Verey (the only Canadian garden featured in *The American Man's Garden*), Penelope Hobhouse (*The Flower Garden*), and Marjorie Harris (*The Canadian Gardener*). Despite this success, George and Bruce recently sold their famous "Bankview" property and have embarked on their third garden project in the city. When I visited them in their new home they had just spent all

Statuary plays an important part in the "Bankview" garden. "Flora" is beautifully placed under a holly tree beside paths leading to and from this shady sitting area.

day in their new garden laying out beds and spreading some of the twenty-two yards of composted topsoil that had just been delivered. George, who is recovering from a heart attack of a year ago, described the making of Bankview.

"Because I was past president of the Victoria Horticultural Society and founding member of the Hallmark Society, it seemed only natural that we would eventually leave our Oak Bay cottage and restore a heritage home," explained George. Historic Bankview, located on a steeply sloping bank overlooking the Gorge waterway, was built in 1893. They chose it for its corner lot and its proximity to George's workplace at the Saxe Point municipal garden. Their award-winning restoration of the house took a year-and-a-half, at which point they began to contemplate the garden. In 1984, the garden was levelled with a backhoe into terraces in a traditional Lutyens and Gertrude Jekyll design, using every inch of garden by removing every bit of grass. "It was essential for us that it work with the architecture of the house," recalled Bruce. "We used a dark stone for the walls, stairs, columns, and pond so that, in the bare bones of winter, it would look like an old stone foundation."

By the spring of 1985, construction work was completed and well-rotted compost and chicken manure added to the existing glacial till. Fine gravel was spread for the paths. Both Bruce and George, passionate and knowledgeable plantsmen, are founding members of the Victoria Horticultural Society's Hardy Plant Group. Their garden began with hostas, ferns, hardy geraniums, and perennials from their Oak Bay garden, as well as choice plants from their friends in the Hardy Plant Study Group. Planting was completed with the thought that viewing would be done from the verandah looking down at the garden, and from their informal seating area under a holly canopy where the charming "Flora" figure was placed amid a carpet of Bowles golden grass (*Milium effusum* 'Aureum'), *Geranium endressii*, and *Corydalis lutea*.

"Our long, narrow Oak Bay garden was designed with a series of well-defined 'rooms' bordered by flowering trees and shrubs," recalled George. In the Bankview garden they also created a series of "rooms" which flowed this time from level to level, bordered by carefully placed columns. "Hot colours such as deep reds were kept separate from the romantic colours such as pinks, purples, and blues," explained Bruce. "Of course green is used as a colour in the design," added George, "but we shy away from bright reds and oranges."

In the Bankview garden, a focal point, or "presence" as George described it, is the magnificent old yew, *Taxus baccata*, which grows at the bottom of the sloped terrace. Below it sat the "white lady" figure surrounded by Bruce's favourite hostas, *Hosta plantaginea* 'Grandiflora,' the almost blue-green *H. sieboldiana*, the white-tipped *H. crispula*, and the golden-centred *H. fortunei* 'Aurea Marginata' (which is a favourite hiding place for the three resident cats, Jessie, Roger, and Martha). In the background, sweet rocket, *Hesperis matronalis*, *Anemone* x *hybrida*, and *Dicentra spectabilis* f. *alba* form a halo of white, while in the foreground *Geranium endressii* echoes the foliage of the anemones and spills over the path. Beside it *Euphorbia characias* subsp. *wulfenii*'s dramatic foliage is an interesting contrast.

Looking back to the verandah, the enormous leaves of the *Petasites japonicus*, and tiny-leafed *Hedera helix* 'Goldheart' rim the pool. Oriental peonies, lady ferns, spiky euphorbias, and hardy geraniums border the gravel, interspersed with clumps of spring tulips; *Iris pseudacorus* rises from the pool. A background of calla lilies, *Zantedeschia aethiopica*, and meadowsweet (*Filipendula palmata*) complete the planting, echoing the vertical line. Everywhere you look, your eye is drawn inward to the dappled light playing on the soft foliage. Statuary and potted plants draw you up the stairs to the clematis-covered (*C. montana*) archway and the rose-covered (*R.* 'Gloire de Dijon') verandah. It is a meticulous garden from planning to execution.

"Our new garden will be completely different," laughed Bruce. Once again they are on a corner lot but this time they will keep the grass as pathways from "room" to "room." Their new house was built in the 1930s and their new garden design will reflect that architectural period, using conifers to accentuate vertical lines and trellises

A strategically placed urn planted with Dracaena *is surrounded by lavender and lamb's ears. In the background, a clematis-covered arbour leads the viewer to the lower terrace.*

for privacy and depth. The statue "Flora" has come with them and will be a background feature.

"Victoria is a city of winds," said George, "and one must keep in mind where the mature trees are situated for the prevailing winds. This house is perfectly sited on the lot. In the evening, the sun hits the white house and throws the heat back to the circular drive." "We will create a terrace there," explained Bruce, rolling out a series of detailed plans. "I think we'll try more colour contrasts this time: green...white...grey...yellow...blue...red...mauve...pink. Because we'll have more heat, I'd like to try more grasses in clumps, such as *Miscanthus*," adds George. "And maybe artemisias, verbenas, and verbascums."

The two men are excited by their new garden but admit they are busy with other community work. George is retired from the Parks Department but is an honourary Director of Government House Garden. Bruce still works full-time as a professional florist, and both men are involved in planning a summer Garden and Flower Festival. They are great advocates of the need for public gardens and last year gave a series of lectures on Gertrude Jekyll's garden design and flower arrangement. Their neighbours are watching the making of this new garden with interest. George Radford and Bruce Gibson-Bean are creating another legacy for the city of gardens.

Ravenhill Herb Farm
The Garden of Noel Richardson and Andrew Yeoman

*A*lstroemerias catch the evening summer light at Ravenhill Herb Farm. Across the path lavender, oregano, thyme and lamb's ears spill out onto the brick path. The path leads to the greenhouse and the terraced vegetable garden.

oel Richardson first saw the property at Ravenhill when her eldest daughter was an infant. "The house was derelict but the view was breathtaking. I remember saying out loud I would love to live here one day." Fifteen years later, Noel saw an ad for the farm in the financial section of the *Calgary Herald.* She and her partner, Andrew Yeoman, flew out the next day and bought it. Three years later they opened Ravenhill Herb Farm and visitors have been coming to their garden by the thousands ever since.

"The garden serves many functions, as a dem-

These boots were made for walking but Noel Richardson's son-in-law couldn't resist planting them with creeping thyme for his "herb crazy" mother-in-law.

onstration garden, teaching garden, and experimental farm," said Andrew, a former teacher and geologist. "We designed it initially to ground the house, which appeared as if it were sliding down the hill. Terracing was the obvious solution." Andrew grassed in part of the circular driveway and built a brick patio on the south-facing slope. A pergola with Chinese wisteria and summer jasmine extends over a raised porch beside the patio where Noel keeps her pots of tender herbs and flowers such as myrtle, scented geraniums, bay, rosemary, oleander, and orchids.

From the patio you can wander past the fragrant summer rose garden across the lawn to the hammock swinging on the huge copper beech tree or climb the steps to the swimming pool bordered by a mature dogwood and Japanese maple intertwined with *Clematis* 'Perle d'Azur.' The main steps up from the patio follow a brick path bordered by a perennial planting of peonies, alstroemeria, delphiniums, and Marguerite daisies following great drifts of narcissus in the spring. Grey lamb's ears and forget-me-nots grow in the full sun as an edging.

On the other side of the path is a locally-carved cedar bench for taking in the magnificent views of Tod Inlet and the Mount Newton Valley. The bench is situated against a backdrop of a mature western red cedar and copper beech; in front is a herb garden of box, bay, oregano, and carnations. To the right is a carved totem by Aubrey La Fortune, a coast Salish native whose mother lives on the adjacent Tsawout Reserve. "We are surrounded by three reserves," said Andrew. "It was important to us to support a living artist, rather than copy European influences. We want our farm to reflect the local landscape.

"The older trees provide the structural framework of the garden," explained Andrew, "but we are governed by the steep site and the exposed rocky terrain. We extended the existing walls to modify microclimates and protect against the southwest gales. The hard edge of the paths and walls are softened by the plant material." Large plantings of thyme drip over the edges of the walls while bowers of lady's-mantle spill over the pathways. "We use the plants for contrasting shape, density, texture, leaf size, and colour," said Andrew. "We change things around in order to find the most suitable location in the garden," he explained. "And for interest," added Noel. Drought-tolerant plants such as artemisia and lavender are an important part of the herb farm as water is the limiting factor. All watering is done by hand in the early morning hours.

A few years ago they built a woolly thyme bench under the shade of a laburnum to commemorate the loss of a dear friend. Stone walls and columns covered in *Rosa* 'New Dawn' separate the formal bricked garden from the more informal terraced hillside. Every raised bed on the hillside is accented with peonies. There are large plantings of fennel, asparagus, arugula, lettuces, tomatoes, squashes, grapes, and annual herbs as well as the cash crops grown under cloches for protection. At the bottom of the hill are a dozen fruit trees, all that remains of the original orchard. Beyond the raised beds and greenhouse are tall Douglas firs which provide shade for fledgling plants. A swing with a view of the valley is used with delight by visiting children.

Children love the farm, for they are fascinated by Noel and Andrew's resident peacocks calling in the fir trees or strutting across the fields. They watch the new lambs gamboling on the hillside or pat the resident goat, Vincent Van, and feed the chickens, and the ducks and geese that swim in the pond by an ivy-covered stone moon gate. Two new puppies, Vita and Josephine, have been added to the menagerie.

Noel and Andrew are committed organic gardeners who compost and mulch throughout the year. It means they cannot grow hybrid tea roses or currant bushes that require spraying, but they do mix herbs with shrubs, perennials, and annuals as an insect repellent. Andrew is a firm believer in green mulches. In the fall he sows a mixture of rye, peas, and fava beans. In the spring he turns the green mulch with a spade to build up the depth of soil and prevent the leeching of nutrients down the steep hillside. Currently, Andrew is writing a book on the growing of herbs and vegetables for west coast kitchens.

A thyme bench overlooks the valley and a planting of santolina, oregano, nepeta and pink mounds of dianthus.

Noel and Andrew supply eight restaurants and two delicatessens with basil, chives, shallots oregano, and tarragon. They grow and sell herbs for culinary and landscaping purposes at their farmgate sales every Sunday, and their garden provides food year-round. Noel teaches cookery classes at Ravenhill and is the author of two cookbooks, *Summer Delights* and *Winter Pleasures*, which describe the use of herbs for cooking. She also writes monthly food columns in *City Foods* magazine and *Western Living*. Her youngest daughter is a professional chef and her eldest daughter runs a mystery book store where Noel works one day a week.

Initially Noel and Andrew looked inward while building Ravenhill. Today they are very generous about sharing their garden. Gardeners, chefs, photographers, artists, journalists, and students flock to the farm. Ravenhill has moved them from the private to the political in their community. Andrew is a member of the Association for the Preservation of Rural Central Saanich. Noel is the Chairperson of the Central Saanich Heritage Advisory Committee and a member of the Police Board. They still like to travel and in the fall leave the farm to their full-time caretaker while they visit gardens and relatives in Europe.

Their plans for the future of Ravenhill include a shady, Japanese-style raised walkway with pots of hostas. Noel laughed, "I still can't resist anything that blooms white and silver." While visiting one evening she showed me with obvious delight a large planting of globe thistles which glowed in the moonlight.

The Garden of Al and Shirley Smith

*A*l and Shirley Smith have terraced an outstanding garden on the southwest face of Mt. Douglas. The sheer scope of their project is enough to take your breath away. In early spring flowering pulsatillas brighten up a phlox-studded rockery. The dwarf conifers give the beds a vertical line.

The scope of Al and Shirley Smith's garden is enough to take your breath away. With over 3,500 labelled species on a terraced, two-acre, west-facing lot overlooking the Blenkinsop Valley, it is a spectacular garden with international appeal.

Gardeners, horticulturists and plant collectors from all over the world come to see the Smiths' on-going creation. The Royal Horticultural Society from Great Britain, Cornell University, the Washington, D.C., Garden Club, and the Seattle Arboretum have all signed the Smiths' guest book, as have international friends and colleagues in the rock and alpine gardening world with whom Al shares seeds. Local garden clubs and horticultural students visit annually to see the garden and pick up tips from Al on plant propagation. The Smiths' lath house contains over ten thousand plants and Al is in the process of building a greenhouse for his thirty to forty flats of pleiones. Their heather collection boasts over four hundred species and a new Irish bell heather Al propagated, 'Silver Bell,' has just been registered.

Al and Shirley witness many new and unusual plant species during the fifty to sixty hours they work in the garden every week. With their keen eyes they have found a double white campanula, a double white narcissus, a white dianthus, and a snowdrop with six petals that looks like a crocus (Al has nicknamed it a "snocus"). Shirley has both a phlox named for her ('Little Shirley') and a rhododendron: 'Shirley Smith' was propagated by a local plantsman, Albert de Mezey. Al Smith has had to slow down for the last three months because of a recent hip replacement, but Shirley has taken up the slack while watering, weeding, mowing, and harvesting the fruits and vegetables.

The summer flowering tuber Roscoea humeana, *of the ginger family, is known to be six to eight inches. In the Smith garden, it is over two feet.*

Al worked thirty-seven years for the Parks Department and Shirley worked for years with a health services agency. They inherited the property from Al's mother and, in 1981, built their West Coast timber house. By 1987 they were both retired and able to focus full-time on their garden. "We originally wanted a small planting around the house," remembered Al, "but maintenance on the rest of the property was too great. The garden just grew like Topsy."

To begin terracing the rocky slope, Al and Shirley hauled rocks up the hill to build rock walls; they also brought in hundreds of yards of gravel for the paths and alpine mix. Al uses a mix of twenty-five percent chip seal (three-eighths of an inch of crushed rock, no fines), twenty-five percent washed sand with peat moss and existing soil. They top dress with thirty-five yards of compost which they generate every year as well as an equal amount in municipal leaf mulch. The Smiths' fertilize with slow-release osmocote. But they do not spray. "Birds and butterflies thrive here," said Al, pointing to hummingbirds and hummingbird moths. "We want to encourage them."

Al and Shirley are great believers in native flora. Garry oak, ocean spray, Oregon grape, kinnickinnick, and native ferns are used throughout the garden and the back section is left wild with native spring lilies. Because the property borders Mount Douglas Park and rural farm land, deer and rabbits are a constant problem. The Smiths' use an electric fence with a nylon monofilament in between. Each year they witness the does showing their new fawns where to walk around the property. Each night Al puts up the fence around the driveway with markers.

Our tour began by the front door where the Smiths have a twenty-foot-high, south-facing *Fredmontodendron californicum* beside heavenly bamboo, yews, golden rain tree (*Koelreuteria paniculata*), dwarf pines, and *Tsuga canadensis* 'Coles Prostrate' amid iris and native plants. The Smiths plan to build a tufa bed here with rocks from their gardening friends, Peter and Marylee Platt. At one corner is a very tall *Dierama pulcherrimum* in which Al has a special interest. He has over a dozen different varieties, one of which is over eight feet high.

We crossed the driveway, passed a new rockery with heathers and alpines to a shady spot under a Garry oak which is a seepage site suitable for Al's pleiones. He pointed out an interesting astilbe collection with deep pink, pale pink, and even white forms beside crested male ferns and *Kirengeshoma palmata* covering a mass planting of spring-time anemones. The Smiths also collect poppies. International poppy expert Christopher Grey Wilson visited the garden last year to take photos of *Papaver beldrictchii*, an apricot-coloured poppy with light grey foliage. Included in his book will be photos of the Smiths' snow poppies, *Eomecon chionantha*, which look identical to bloodroot. There are also several other meconopsis in the garden, including a relatively new hybrid with four-inch gentian blue flowers: *M. x sheldonii.*

We followed the gravel paths to a sunny border with creeping thyme dripping over the rocks. Of interest was the *Parrotia persica* with a deep red *Penstemon gloxinioides* and a purple *P. hirsutus* 'Pygmaeus.' Across the path *Tropaeolum speciosum*, the flame creeper, was taking over both a large ocean spray and *Acanthus speciosum* beside a beautiful specimen of the ginger family, *Roscoea humeana*. Toad lilies, hydrangeas, mock orange, and one of the few roses in the Smith collection, the bush 'Sweetheart,' bloomed prolifically.

On the northern border *Stewartia pseudocamellia* with large papery white flowers and deep yellow centres stood out among summer flowering tree heathers, Russian sage, and hebes. In the new rockery, insects buzzed in the showy *Gentiana acaulis*, *G. sino-ornata* 'Kingfisher,' the compact shrub *Daphne collina*, and the unusual *Penstemon rupicola* 'Alba.' At the end of the rockery the Smiths' double campanulas bloomed blue and white under a silver pear tree.

In front of the house are small conifers for accent which Al salvaged from demolition sales. He pointed out the Japanese coffin tree, *Juniperus recurva* var. *coxii* which has interesting bark and soft foliage. Beside it, the rare *Franklinia alatamaha* bloomed; it is only known in arboreta, having been made extinct in the wild. Its blooms are similar to Stewartia. One of Shirley's favourite shrubs is *Scrophularia*

nodusa, or variegated mint, with deep red flowers that do not die back in the winter. Birds love it and the foliage is ideal for arrangements.

On a dry rocky outcrop Al and Shirley have a large sedum and sempervivum bed that slowly feeds off the gravel. Wherever we walked the Smiths showed me unusual trees, shrubs, and rockery plants. They do not segregate colours. "All colours are part of nature," said Al, who chooses sites for plants according to optimum growing conditions. Below the house are perennial borders terraced to the driveway with plantings of coreopsis, scented bud-dleias, a dwarf hypericum from Egypt, and a collection of grasses including the Russian native, *Stipa barbata*. In the past the Smiths used to plant up to four thousand annuals each year. This year, they are extending the shrub borders for ease of maintenance. It would take many visits before a keen observer could absorb even half of what this garden offers.

Al and Shirley are preparing a lecture and slide presentation about their garden because of an invitation from the Ontario Rock and Alpine Society. Their talk is aptly titled, "The Garden That Never Ends."

The Garden of George and Isabel Straith

Under a canopy of mature Garry oak is the Straith garden originally planted sixty years ago. The front wrought iron gate is flanked by cedar hedging, Hydrangea macrophylla *and azaleas from Exbury in England.*

Walking up the driveway to the Straith home and garden is not for the faint of heart. The property rises sharply from the already steep road to a height of land where a dramatic view of the Olympic Mountains and the Strait of Juan de Fuca awaits you. The bones of the garden were planted sixty years ago by George Straith's parents. Isabel Straith continues to look after the garden with a little help from her sons.

"This was a great garden in which to raise our four boys," Isabel recalled. "They clambered over the rocks and played ball where the driveway circles [the only flat area on the property]. I was intimidated at first taking on my mother-in-law's garden, but slowly, over time, we learned which plants were weeds and which were not." Since then, Isabel has always gardened, although, during the years that she worked full-time in the family clothing business, she had fewer hours to do so. Today, one of Isabel's sons lives nearby and offers his time. She also has professional help one half-day a week and enjoys working in the garden herself every day. "It is good therapy for me," said Isabel, who looks as fit and glamorous as a woman half her age.

When the Straiths inherited the garden in the 1950s, there were five mature rhododendron 'Pink Pearl' bushes at the front entrance of the house. They remained, but the east-facing rockery planted with heathers, rock roses, white-scented broom, and saxifrages has been rebuilt as one large perennial bed; white calla lilies, *Iris ochroleuca*, and *I. pseudacorus* thrived among the rhododendrons while aubrieta, arabis, arctic willow, thrift, and periwinkle spilled over the rocks. In full sun are grey *Erica tetralix* 'Alba Mollis,' *Tan-*

Isabel Straith practises Japanese flower arranging and this is very evident in her choice of flowers and plant forms. In a shady corner the round blossoms of the hydrangea are in contrast to the pink spikes of the astilbe, while Japanese anemones provide contrasting foliage.

acetum densum subsp. *amani*, grey woolly thyme, sedums, deep purple dianthus, and *Sisyrinchium graminoides* with deep blue and yellow flowers. Dwarf Japanese maples, a tall willow gentian, and a tiny rock gentian are from the original rockery.

"We had to take out the four ball-shaped cedars on either side of the stairs because they became too large." The cotoneaster and Virginia creeper climbing on the house, originally planted in the 1930s, were replaced by *Wisteria sinensis* and *Clematis armandii*. The house faces due east with enormous rock outcrops protecting it from the southwest winds, but the bitter northeast wind in winter, especially the winter of 1989, did considerable damage to the garden. "We lost clematis, several rhododendrons, and rockery plants but the old Japanese maples survived," Isabel remembered. "The American Rhododendron Society visited the next spring and we worked very hard to replace the rhododendrons and other shrubs. The azaleas are all the original Exbury varieties from England."

From the main entrance a wide gravel path descends to a level lawn with a curved bench for sitting under the shade of *Magnolia campbellii*. Slate stairs descend to the "sunken rose garden" which was originally located in front of the magnolia. There are a few original roses left such as 'Chicago,' 'Fragrant Cloud,' 'Peace,' and 'Elizabeth.' Isabel has added 'Christian Dior' and other hybrids as the old roses died off.

Following a narrow grass path to the shady bottom of the garden are lacecap hydrangeas, pink astilbes, many species of large-leafed hostas, and an interesting collection of native and introduced ferns. Isabel practises Japanese flower arranging and her aesthetic sense is evident in this beautiful planting where the textures of rock, leaf, and flower are never overstated. Beside it, a continuous planting of marsh marigolds pours down the hill within a rock crevice. Isabel prefers whites, pinks, purples, and blue colours in the garden, but she admits the swath of yellow marigold flowers in early spring is a welcome sight. She can contain their invasive habit between the rocks.

Over the years, as the oaks grew and provided more shade, the Straiths removed the areas of sparse grass and planted more rhododendrons, hydrangeas, and hostas. Isabel's own mother was a great gardener and, in her honour, a large drift of shade-loving lily-of-the-valley, her favourite flower, was planted. In sunnier locations, large ornamental conifers such as Mugo pine, umbrella pine, weeping larch, yew, and dwarf blue spruce are placed as focal points.

Climbing up the steep driveway we pass two enormous, mature Douglas firs that Isabel has pruned spirally. It is a more long-lasting and effective method of pruning large trees than the old method of topping. Climbing up one of the trees is *Clematis paniculata* which Isabel prunes annually to maintain its vigorous blooms in the fall. At the end of the driveway, under the shade of the old-growth firs, Isabel's son has built a curved slate patio with a slate bench. In the background, native ocean spray, salal, and *Rhododendron* 'Jean-Marie Montague' are planted with candelabra primulas, hostas, and hellebores in the foreground. Between the cracks of the slate was creeping thyme. The sound of a fountain nearby added to the ambience.

Up the steps to a side porch is an enormous vine of Dutchman's Pipe, *Aristolochia elegans*, which Isabel trained as a screen from the wind. The Straiths hauled hundreds of wheelbarrows full of fill and rock to build a large stone patio against the rock hill. Shaded by a mature ornamental plum and the twisted branches of the Garry oak we paused to sit. "The strengths of this garden are in the rock and gnarled oaks," said Isabel, smiling. "We have tried as much as possible to let the natural elements dictate the planting." It is a beautiful garden, with all the warmth and grace of its owner.

*C*ampanulas, ferns, hostas and a blue spruce vie for space in a shady rock outcrop. "The strengths of this garden are in the rock and gnarled oaks," said Isabel Straith.

The Garden of Peter Symcox and Fernand Choquette

_P_eter Symcox and Fernand Choquette used their expertise in television production to design a terraced garden on a sheer rocky cliff. The garden is jam-packed with self-seeded perennials including aubretia, rock soapwort (Saponaria ocymoides), helianthemum, arabis and the tall spikes of Euphorbia characias _subsp._ wulfenii.

*I*n Victoria you do not have to fly to Europe to feel the Mediterranean. A short drive to Metchosin to the house of Peter Symcox and Fernand Choquette will transport you to a sunnier climate, relaxed conversation, and never-ending vistas. Sunglasses and straw hats are a must on the slate terrace. Their home, perched on a height of land and bathed in sun, has an uninterrupted view from Clover Point to William Head. Their garden, full to overflowing with sun-loving and drought-resistant plants, emerged from the scorched hillside in truly operatic fashion.

*D*rought resistant varieties are essential in this sun-baked garden. A potted geranium is surrounded by lavender, rosemary, dianthus, rock roses and a tall tree heather. Shrubs include the native oceanspray (Holodiscus discolor) beside the deep-red leaves of a smoke bush.

Peter and Fernand, both former television directors from Montreal (Peter in opera and Fernand in documentary), had the perfect talents to tackle this mammoth job. They had left their twenty-five acres in Vermont, complete with four acres of cultivated woodlands and meadows, to retire to a simpler life on the west coast. It was chance that led them to their new house two months after their arrival, and a whim that got them thinking, perhaps, they would have a small garden. Faced with a twenty-foot dropping slope of bedrock and grassy knolls, Peter and Fernand hired help.

Enter Richard's Landscaping and Hardrock Masonry. Richard and crew marked out paths on the grass with a spray can of white paint. They scraped what soil there was to bare rock, sifting out the native wild onion bulblets and *Brodiaea* bulbs. Peter and Fernand laugh when they recall the next step. "Then the fun really began," they recall. In the fall several truck loads of stones were delivered and dropped into place by a series of wooden chutes and brute strength. Hardrock Masonry built curved retaining walls. Finally, twelve yards of topsoil and five yards of gravel were hauled, trundled, and carried down the slope. A special soil mixture high in grit and suitable for alpines and drought-tolerant plants was mixed for the new beds and coarse gravel was laid for the paths. Then Peter and Fernand sat back and waited for spring to plant.

Within a week it had begun to rain. "It poured solidly for three days and nights. Folks were flooded out up-Island, mud slides blocked mountain roads," remembers Peter with a shudder. "And our little paths, so carefully planned and executed, became gullies through which the water rushed with reckless glee. Dismayed, we surveyed the wreckage."

It was a friend who suggested a way out of the mess. A series of stone steps placed strategically would act as a waterfall, slowing down the rush of water and allowing it time to seep into the soil. The steps worked beautifully and Peter and Fernand have not looked back since. "If anything, we have to keep cutting back plants because the growth has been tremendous," said Peter. "Friends had given us so

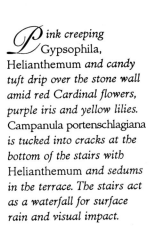

$\mathcal{P}$ink creeping Gypsophila, Helianthemum and candy tuft drip over the stone wall amid red Cardinal flowers, purple iris and yellow lilies. Campanula portenschlagiana is tucked into cracks at the bottom of the stairs with Helianthemum and sedums in the terrace. The stairs act as a waterfall for surface rain and visual impact.

many cuttings and bits of plants that we soon ran out of room." Another friend named their catch-all garden at the bottom of the hill, beyond the woodland walk, the "crazy" garden.

This so-called crazy garden is anything but. It is a collection of bulbs, perennials, and old roses that would not otherwise grow in the hot terraces or in the small rhododendron garden surrounding the house. Daylilies, lupins, irises, poppies, and bergamot grow in early summer following the spring narcissus and tulips. In the late summer foxgloves, daisies, and montbretia tangle decoratively among the herbs tarragon, basil, oregano, and heliotrope. Bordering the garden is a trellis of roses that includes *Rosa* 'New Dawn,' 'Cécile Brunner,' 'Altissimo,' 'Veilchenblau,' and 'Kiftsgate.' Shaded by arbutus and pine trees, this is a peaceful spot in late summer to sit and repose. "It is not 'crazy,'" declared Peter, "but more of a haven from the noise and confusion of the outside world." Fernand smiled in agreement.

"Like all gardens," Peter explained, "this one is an amalgam, a blend of ideas, enthusiasm, and downright hard work, with so many people making their own personal contribution and suggestions. It is all very well to have ideas but the real de-

light came from the creative input of those who helped so willingly to transform the mental image of rock, plant, and soil." Peter and Fernand were recently awarded "Gardener of the Year" by *Canadian Gardening* magazine for their garden design.

Today Peter and Fernand have help from Kenny Jones, trained at Victoria's Horticultural Centre of the Pacific, to maintain their garden. They are very conscious of depth and foreground, having worked in television. They want to keep an interesting object in the forefront while maintaining background "drama." It is like an opera, one that is always being fine tuned.

Back up the steps past the potted sempervivums and geraniums leads to the top terrace. Aubrieta, allysum, gypsophila, and helianthemum spill over the rock walls while lavender, arabis, sedums, and dianthus are tucked in hot spots. Heathers, peonies, azaleas, and lilies grow in the deeper soil pockets at the edges of the terrace under the shade of the arbutus trees. A wooden bench is the perfect seat for the magnificent view. The two gardeners admit that they often have memories of a villa in Capri. But they do not have to go anywhere to experience the feel of the Mediterranean.

The Garden of Jack Todd

*V*isitors come from all over the world to see the Todds' collection of rhododendrons, alpines, annuals and bonsai. This garden has year-round colour.

When Jack Todd bought the spectacular property overlooking the Strait of Juan de Fuca and the Olympic Range, he told his wife they were not going to have a garden, just a few bulbs. That was twenty years ago. Today, their house is surrounded by magnificent vistas and year-round colour.

Jack knew the property well before he bought it, having been raised a few hundred metres away in the house at the bottom of the hill. The property was owned by the doctor who delivered Jack into the world. After the doctor's death, his two daughters lived in the old stone mansion for another seventy-five years but circumstances required them to subdivide and sell the wild, rocky promontory. Jack bought one portion and the municipality bought the rest as a park because of its mountain views and spring wild flowers.

In keeping with his original plan Jack did plant bulbs, hundreds of them, but then, like Topsy, the garden began to grow. Soon rock walls and paths were built and two hundred yards of topsoil were spread. His garden today is roughly divided into three sections. A lower garden of rhododendrons, perennial borders, and annuals surrounds mature Garry oak trees. A mid-garden consists of terraced stone walls with azaleas, smaller rhododendrons, and conifers. Finally, there is an upper garden of rock and alpine plants that can withstand the constant buffeting of the prevailing wind blowing across the Strait of Juan de Fuca. There are ponds at various levels of the garden stocked with water lilies and fish.

Wind is the limiting factor for everything Jack grows. He uses large native *Thuja* (cedars) as a windbreak and the smaller upright California

Hostas surround a fountain amid the early spring blooms of pansies, forget-me-nots, narcissus, daffodils, rhododendrons and a deep-pink camellia. Jack Todd is not afraid to mix colours.

113

Juniperus tortulosa. This juniper has softer foliage than our native variety and thrives in salt spray. It is an excellent ornamental because it stays relatively small and forms interesting twisted shapes. Native *Pinus contorta* is also wind resistant and features prominently on the north side of the garden. Jack collected most of his pine specimens in the wild where he also picked up local slate shale. "I am always on the lookout for plants and rocks," he mused. "If I see a rhodo I like or one I've never seen before I'm not afraid to knock on the owner's door and ask for a cutting. I take the cuttings to a local nursery for propagation because I don't have a greenhouse. I've collected dianthus (pinks) this way and I'm a great nursery hopper, always looking for new plants."

Jack is a great believer in colour and his garden is vibrant year round. "I use bright colours in shady spots and softer tones in sunlight," Jack explains. He is not afraid to use annuals in mass plantings, which he alters every year because he doesn't like "sameness." Jack has help twice a week from a knowledgeable horticulturist who maintains the grounds, spreads compost, and handles the re-lentless task of watering. Because of the rock a watering system was not possible and so most watering is done with hoses on timers. Even Jack's extensive native bonsai collection must be watered daily in the hot dry days of summer.

Statuary features prominently in the garden. Bronze herons wade in the lily ponds, Buddhas meditate in leafy corners, and two children examining a bird seem real on their rocky perch. The latter sculpture was made by local artist Peggy Walton Packard. It provides a focal point and gives the garden a human scale.

But gardening is only part of Jack Todd's life. When he is not gardening, or playing golf, or teaching the blind to swim, Jack will get up in the wee hours of the morning and drive to the north end of Vancouver Island for mountain climbing. His latest trip up 3,500-metre Mount Elkhorn was thwarted a few hundred metres from the summit but he returned in the Fall and tried again, this time successfully. "My thighs were so sore and tired that I couldn't step into the van but had to kneel to get in. It was the toughest climb I have ever done but," he added with a twinkle, "so exhilarating."

*A*lpine plants *Gentiana acoulis, Armeria caespitosa, Iris verna and Pulsatilla vulgaris bloom profusely despite being constantly buffeted by prevailing winds from the Strait of Juan de Fuca.*

The Garden of Nick and Evelyn Weesjes

*N*ick and Evelyn Weesjes have created the ten-acre garden at "Towner Crest" from scratch. In the Douglas fir forest, Evelyn seeded candelabra primulas in a damp gully amid a backdrop of hybrid and species rhododendrons.

To visit the ten-acre garden of Nick and Evelyn Weesjes is to enter another world. Driving through the front gates, you enter a forest of second-growth Douglas fir and Grand fir with big-leafed maples, cascara, and red alder in shady, wet sites and arbutus and yews in drier areas. Na-tive woodland shrubs such as ocean spray, huck-leberries, and Oregon grape are evident but the main feature of the garden are the magnificent species and hybrid rhododendrons.

Nick and Evelyn bought the property in 1972 and started a small nursery of plants at Evelyn's

Pleiones raised from seed thrive in the mossy forest floor of "Towner Crest." They were given to the Weesjeses by another devoted gardening couple, Al and Shirley Smith.

parents' house. They both worked at the University of British Columbia (UBC) Botanical Gardens. Nick, the son of a Dutch greenhouse grower, worked in the six-hundred-acre gardens at UBC from 1949 to 1981 and was head gardener for twenty-five of his thirty-two-and-a-half years there. Evelyn worked as a plant propagator and received a gold medal from the American Rhododendron Society for her work in propagating over 338 species rhododendrons from gardens in Britain. They moved to Vancouver Island in the fall of 1981 and began the task of clearing the site.

Nick and Evelyn started on the north side first. With a mattock and shovel, they dug out salal and trailing blackberries. Dead debris was burned. Leaving the stumps for the pileated woodpeckers, they maintained much of the native understorey. Each section of the garden was prepared meticulously, separated by wide, well-planned trails where two people can comfortably walk side by side. Over one hundred yards of soil were brought in to add to the existing clay and each plant was heavily mulched with compost, peat moss, and bark mulch. A watering system was put in by Nick, plant by plant, section by section. Today, there are eight acres under cultivation, comprising forty-five planted sections; all were developed, planted, and maintained by Nick and Evelyn, alone.

Their house, a modest rancher, was built on the edge of a wet area that would not have been a good area for planting. Nick built a charming brick-bordered pond by the house that is home to waterlilies and visiting raccoons. The Weesjeses respect animals on their property. One resident deer used to lick their pet rabbit on the head. They welcome river otters that come up from the beach and play in the pond. A raccoon washed his hands in the water while I visited and did not seem to mind the four resident cats.

Near the house, Nick has built a lath house for the fledgling rhododendrons and azaleas, many of which started as cuttings from estates in England and Scotland. The lath house looks like a small nursery, with pots of rhododendron hybrids, deciduous shrubs, lilies, and perennial seedlings. Their greenhouse is packed with hundreds of ge-

raniums and pelargoniums which Evelyn grows for the University of Victoria plant sale. Their vegetable garden is modest by comparison, but they do grow peas, beans, lettuce, and squash surrounded by a lattice fence dripping in many species of clematis. "We are not wealthy," said Evelyn with a laugh, "but we *are* healthy."

It is hard to imagine the scope of their undertaking but they work bit by bit, all day, every day. "You have to love it," said Evelyn, smiling at Nick, "and we do." "Towner Crest," the Weesjes property, was named after the original settler, William Towner, a hops farmer. Evelyn remembers as a child walking past the oast houses where the hops were dried. She has since named one of her hybrids 'Towner Crest' (parents: *Rhododendron* 'Van Nes Sensation' x *R.* 'Mrs. H. Fogg').

Evelyn does not only propagate rhododendrons. She sprinkles seeds everywhere. She tried to seed *Primula japonica* in a damp gully but the creek flooded that year, washing away all her seedlings. She tried again and the result is a dramatic spring covering of pale-pink to deep-red candelabra primulas. Star flowers and sword ferns mingle in the understorey. Birds chatter in the tree tops and bathe in the streams. The forest floor absorbs the sounds in a tranquil stillness.

On the southern side of the house, the land slopes down towards a creek where the landscape is less cultivated and more wild. Evelyn has added trilliums, primulas, calla lilies, and hostas to the indigenous ostrich ferns and skunk cabbage. A hand-hewn bridge lies over a shallow waterfall that becomes a raging torrent during spring flooding. Looking up you cannot but be humbled by the enormous trees swaying in the wind. "It is the trees that make the garden," said Nick. "They are more important to us than anything else. As they grow the garden changes, and that is what is so interesting."

"You need a garden of this size to grow some of the large species rhododendrons," explained Nick. Their foliage is very large with huge, glossy, leathery leaves that are often brown and woolly underneath. Nick and Evelyn have systematically separated the larger species from the smaller hy-

Each section of the garden was prepared meticulously, separated by wide, well-planned trails where two people can comfortably walk side by side.

brid rhododendrons with plantings of deciduous shrubs such as cherries, azaleas, and hydrangeas for early and late spring colour. Evelyn has marked each plant with a name marker. With over 3,500 plants, this is a daunting task in itself, one of many that they do willingly and with cheerful vigour.

Nick and Evelyn are members of the Rhododendron Society and the Hardy Plant Group of the Victoria Horticultural Society. They share plants with other gardeners, showing with pride a spec-

tacular collection of pleiones which Al and Shirley Smith, another devoted gardening couple, had given them. Evelyn is slowly building up a collection of perennials for the "edges" of each section.

Both Nick and Evelyn are very gracious about people coming to visit the garden. Gardeners, painting groups, fundraising tours, and individuals are all welcome while Nick and Evelyn continue their work. Every day it is a labour of love.

The Garden of Norma Wilson

*N*orma Wilson is a devoted gardener who is constantly adding to and rearranging her garden. She extended the existing narrow borders to two points and accented them with dwarf vertical conifers. A curved bench overlooks a lily pond and an "occupied" birdhouse.

I took up gardening seriously when I retired as a physiotherapist in 1986, and I must say I have never worked so hard in my life. The digging, the hauling, and the lifting. It's a good thing I was a physio and strong," smiled Norma Wilson in her conservatory overlooking the blossom-laden trees in her two-thirds-of-an-acre garden. "When I was a physio I talked to people. Now I talk to plants."

"When we moved in the '60s, the lawn was weedy and lumpy and the garden was very open. My Cornish mother was a great gardener and loved rhododendrons. I made my first mistake by planting too many rhododendrons to fill in the space. Then I went back to England and saw the rhododendron collection at the Edmund Rothschilde garden in Exbury. When I returned home I just stood at the bottom of the garden and stared. It was then that I began to see my own garden. It was obvious to me

that the space needed to be divided up so that you did not see everything at once."

Mrs. Wilson extended her flowering shrub borders to two points and accented them with dwarf conifers and rocks salvaged from a road-building crew. By changing the lines of the garden it draws the eye out and beckons the viewer. She placed the pendulous trees over her exposed bedrock bluff while maintaining the large vertical Garry oaks, dogwood, and plums in the main garden. The shadows in this garden are a constant source of interest.

"It is a formal garden, with cluttered cosy corners," laughed Norma. A few years ago a pergola with *Rosa* 'Félicité et Perpétue' and *Clematis armandii* was built to lead you into the garden from the front gate. A pond followed, with bronze Malaysian herons and adjoining bird houses that

A pergola leads from the front gate to the house with Rosa *'Félicité and Perpétue' and* Clematis armandii. *Chinese lanterns and dragon pots are added features.*

are "fully occupied." Norma's summer house has been expanded with a brick walkway and rose-covered pergola. The biggest job that Norma and her husband Gerald tackled was replacing all the fencing. They had to clean out the entire perimeter of the garden and, now that the garden is clean, there are fewer pests. She doesn't spray but feeds her garden annually with a mixture of leaf mulch, compost, and cow manure.

"We are lucky in Victoria to have had wonderful gardening matriarchs. I have a lovely *Paeony mlokosewitschii*, the pale lemon-coloured one, that the late Sybil McCulloch gave me. Her *Cardiocrinum giganteum*, the white trumpet lily, is bigger than I am. And Sheila Anderson's sempervivums are in a special corner that I dedicate to her. These were generous women who shared their plants and their wisdom.

"I don't draw pictures and plans—every year it is different," said Norma apologetically. "But am always looking, learning, and intrigued by what is growing around me. I don't have colour schemes, I blend with my eye—it's very personal. Green is still the most important colour. I love the green of spring," she sighs, gazing out her window. "I have started making trough gardens and am more and more interested in alpines and propagation but they are time-consuming." Norma has a greenhouse and lath house which she plans to use for alpine seedlings to fill up her new rock garden. She has just replaced a small stretch of lawn with a knot garden to cut down on summer watering.

Time is a crucial factor in Norma Wilson's life. As president of the Victoria Horticultural Society she must meet the demands of a society that is growing by leaps and bounds, with an annual membership of 1,500 families. She must balance the needs of an older membership gardening in smaller spaces and a young membership gardening for the first time with large spaces but little time and money. Mrs. Wilson is also a founding director of the Greater Victoria Gardeners Association, which is planning its first annual Chelsea-style flower show. "We all volunteer our time," she explained, while handling yet another phone call about an executive meeting.

A rustic bird bath is surrounded by spring-flowering azaleas. Norma describes her garden as "formal with cluttered cosy corners."

"My husband, a physician, retires next year. He's a great help fixing things. I'm sure we will spend more time in this garden then. All these projects keep me in shape. It is all the little anticipations that make you thrive. Five years ago I bought a tiny *Rhododendron macabeanum* which is supposed to flower after twenty years and grow forty-five-feet high. I'll wait. I wish I could grow vegetables here but it is too shady. Still, in the summer to sit in my summer house and watch the wind playing with the trees and the ever-changing shadows...it is lovely. Last summer friends celebrated a golden wedding anniversary here and recently neighbours used our garden for their wedding photos. I love it here. This was the old Pemberton house. Lots of families have been raised here. I feel happy now raising plants."